The Inspiration, Please!
Trivia Quiz Book

The Inspiration, Please! Trivia Quiz Book

1,173 QUESTIONS AND ANSWERS ABOUT RELIGION,
BASED ON TELEVISION'S ONLY GAME SHOW WITH A FAITH LIFT

Edited by Donald K. Epstein and Linda Hanick
*with an Introduction by Television Host
Robert G. Lee*

Quill
WILLIAM MORROW AND COMPANY, INC.
NEW YORK

Copyright © 1997 by Parish of Trinity Church of New York City

All rights reserved. No part of this book may be reproduced or utilized in any form or by any means, electronic or mechanical, including photocopying, recording, or by any information storage or retrieval system, without permission in writing from the Publisher. Inquiries should be addressed to Permissions Department, William Morrow and Company, Inc., 1350 Avenue of the Americas, New York, N.Y. 10019.

It is the policy of William Morrow and Company, Inc., and its imprints and affiliates, recognizing the importance of preserving what has been written, to print the books we publish on acid-free paper, and we exert our best efforts to that end.

Library of Congress Cataloging-in-Publication Data

The inspiration, please! trivia quiz book : 1,173 questions and answers about religion, based on television's only game show with a faith lift / edited by Donald K. Epstein and Linda Hanick ; with an introduction by Robert G. Lee.
    p.   cm.
  ISBN 0-688-15149-3
  1. Religions—Miscellanea.   I. Epstein, Donald K.   II. Hanick, Linda.
BL85.I67   1997
200—dc21   97-24149
                                                                       CIP

Printed in the United States of America

First Edition

1 2 3 4 5 6 7 8 9 10

BOOK DESIGN BY MICHAEL MENDELSOHN

**To Ruth, Jack, Anne, and our families . . .
for filling our lives with inspiration**

Welcome to Inspiration, Please!

Religion often gets a bad rap these days, and television has to take some of the blame. In the 1970s and 1980s, much of the religious programming on TV consisted of Bible-thumping evangelists "curing" the sick while pleading for contributions, or glib preachers in cozy, talk-show settings smilingly warning that *their* beliefs are the *only* beliefs. Thankfully, those images are receding as a new kind of religious TV programming is beginning to take hold—programming that affirms diversity and honors the spiritual search. It's in this new climate that television's first religious game show, *Inspiration, Please!* was born.

We call it "the only game show with a faith lift," and, all punning aside, the goal of *Inspiration, Please!*, since it went on the air on October 1, 1995, has been to try, in an entertaining and informative way, to make religion an enjoyable part of everyday life. We think religion—ours, yours, and everybody else's—is purposeful, important, and serious. But we think it can be fun, too.

Another aim of the show (and this book) is to introduce people to the religious traditions of their neighbors, from those who are members of the Assemblies of God to those who practice Zen Buddhism. Until people stop fighting over whose God is the real God and accept the fact that diversity

Welcome to *Inspiration, Please!*

is a plus, learning something about the other guy's religion has to be a step in the right direction.

And we ought to know a thing or two about diversity. Our show is produced by Trinity Church, Wall Street (Episcopalian); our creative and production team includes men and women of at least a few dozen faiths; and the show is broadcast on the Odyssey Channel, owned by Liberty Media Corporation and the National Interfaith Cable Coalition, a consortium of sixty-five Protestant, Catholic, Jewish, and Eastern Orthodox faith groups.

Like the TV series on which it's based, this book features questions about all faiths, as well as about music, art, movies, theater, literature, folklore, history, famous people, and even sports, proving that religion is indeed everywhere. We try to make the questions fun (it is, after all, a game show) without trivializing or being disrespectful. Our TV contestants have included bus drivers, lawyers, bakers, teachers, accountants, police officers, computer operators, musicians, city planners, and salespeople, among scores of other occupations, as well as a few priests, ministers, rabbis, nuns, deacons, church elders, and seminarians. And they all tell us they never knew that increasing their knowledge of all things religious could be so much fun.

On the following pages you'll find thirty quizzes based on the TV show (each made up of fifteen questions, fifteen bonus questions, and an Inspiration Word puzzle) and complete instructions on how to play the game. Whether you tackle the quizzes by yourself, with a friend, or with a group of friends or family, be prepared for a surprise: If you're like most people, you know a lot more about religion than you think.

—Donald K. Epstein
Linda Hanick
New York

A Few Words of
Thanks

Both the television and quiz book versions of *Inspiration, Please!* are possible only because of an enormous contribution of time and talent by dozens of professional people. Our very special thanks to . . .

Jeff Weber, the man with the original idea for a religious game show and the executive producer who guided it through a maze of development phases into reality.

Robert G. Lee, host of the television series. When he's not at his podium in our Trinity Place TV studio in downtown Manhattan, Robert travels around the country performing his unique stand-up comedy routines based on religion and the Bible. He's also made several hilarious videos. His own deeply held religious beliefs, combined with his wonderful sense of fun, make him the ideal emcee of *Inspiration, Please!*

Bruce Burmester, our TV director. When we first called Bruce, a game-show wizard, an Emmy winner for *The $25,000 Pyramid,* and a good friend for more than twenty years, he did what good friends always do. He dropped everything, flew from his home in sunny California to snowy New York, designed all of our bells, whistles, timing, and scoring devices, and began directing the show in the cool, unflappable Burmester manner. It's conceivable we could do the show without him, but we don't want to think about it.

Rae Pichon, associate producer and contestant coordinator, who per-

---- **A Few Words of Thanks** ----

forms her many jobs better than most people can handle just one. She came to us directly from *Family Feud,* to which we will forever be thankful.

Debbie Mackler, who, in her capacity as associate producer of the show, manages to provide all the glue it takes to hold it together. She is always there, usually at least a step or two ahead of the rest of us.

Phil Dougharty, a human religious encyclopedia who checks and rechecks all of the show's material for accuracy and finds minuscule errors of fact and/or interpretation that even the most astute biblical scholar would probably overlook.

Our Research Staff, who keep us supplied with an endless variety of innovative questions. If you think it's easy, try coming up with one hundred questions a week, each and every week, for approximately forever.

Doris Cooper, editor extraordinary at William Morrow and Company, who guided us expertly through the development and writing stages of this book.

Bill Adler, who saw an article on *Inspiration, Please!* on the front page of *The Wall Street Journal* and immediately thought, "That's a book!" He should know: Bill has not only agented scores of best-sellers by everyone from presidents to unknowns, he's also written and edited dozens of his own.

All the folks at Trinity Church, Wall Street, who supported the creation and development of the show from the very beginning, especially the Reverend Dr. Daniel Paul Matthews, Rector Herbert Donovan, and David Jette.

All of our past religious instructors, who would be so proud.

Contents

Welcome to *Inspiration, Please!* ... vii
A Few Words of Thanks ... ix
My Bias Toward the Pious, by Robert G. Lee ... xiii
How to Play *Inspiration, Please!* ... xvii

THEMED QUIZZES

Quiz #1	You Don't Have to Be Catholic . . .	1
Quiz #2	You Don't Have to Be Jewish . . .	8
Quiz #3	You Don't Have to Be Protestant . . .	15
Quiz #4	Eastern Standard	22
Quiz #5	Quid Pro Quote	29
Quiz #6	Old Testamentality	36
Quiz #7	New Testamentality	43
Quiz #8	Drawing a Blank	50
Quiz #9	That's Entertainment	57
Quiz #10	Animal Crackers	64
Quiz #11	It's All Relative	71
Quiz #12	Hit or Myth	78
Quiz #13	Food for Thought	85
Quiz #14	Book Review	92
Quiz #15	Words and Music	99

CONTENTS

MIXED BAGS

Quiz #16	This and That and Wise Men, Too	106
Quiz #17	Murderers, Angels, Etc.	113
Quiz #18	Let's Get Theory-ous	120
Quiz #19	Is There a Doctrine in the House?	127
Quiz #20	Age-Old Questions	134
Quiz #21	Major Leagues and Minor Prophets	141
Quiz #22	Plagues and Other Fun Stuff	148
Quiz #23	Heretic, There a Tic	155
Quiz #24	Any Way You Slice It (or Cubit)	162
Quiz #25	Statues Without Limitations	169
Quiz #26	By the Numbers	176
Quiz #27	Women, Men, and Other Characters	183
Quiz #28	From Saints to Sinners	190
Quiz #29	Backward and Forward	197
Quiz #30	For Better or Verse	204

About the Editors	211
If You'd Like to Be a Contestant	213
About Trinity Church	214
About Odyssey	215

My Bias Toward The Pious

by Robert G. Lee
TV Host of *Inspiration, Please!*

As a Christian comedian, I'm often asked if I think God has a sense of humor. I think the obvious answer is that He made *us*. Get out of the shower tomorrow morning, look in the mirror, and tell me that God doesn't have a flair for comedy!

I could never be disrespectful when it comes to religion, but I've always been able to find its humorous side. The trouble is that because religion has its solemn aspects, some people take it too seriously. But learning about religion doesn't have to be serious. Anyone who ever had a good Sunday school teacher knows that, and I hope we're proving it again on the *Inspiration, Please!* TV show and in this quiz book.

I've been around religion my whole life. I was raised in the Midwest in a Presbyterian household, and one of my earliest memories is of my Great-Grammy telling me Bible stories while I sat on her knee. She seemed so old I figured she probably knew Jesus, and I thought her stories were so wonderful because she was telling them firsthand.

When I was in the seventh grade, my mother became a Charismatic and I realized that religion can really shake up a family. While Dad remained the staunch Presbyterian, Mom would praise God if the mail showed up on time. When they went to see *The Exorcist,* Mom came home and went around the house casting out demons. It's a wonder she let my brother and me stay.

My Bias Toward the Pious

As a teenager I learned about the New Age movement when one of my cousins claimed that in a past life she was present at the birth of Christ. To this day it seems to me that everyone who believes in reincarnation was around at that time. Bethlehem must have been packed. No wonder there was no room at the inn.

The most startling religious revelation of my life came when I discovered that my best friend, who was Jewish, didn't celebrate Christmas. I was shocked. Like most kids, I didn't pay much attention to the holiness of the holiday, being concerned only with the presents. And here was my very best friend trapped in a family that refused to give him Christmas gifts. I felt a little better when he told me he got a Chanukah present every day for eight days, but I still thought he was deprived until I saw the unbelievable haul he made at his bar mitzvah. I promptly went home and told my parents I wanted to go to Hebrew school, too.

When it came to girls, I was very shy, and for a time I became a kind of agnostic. I believed girls existed—I just had no personal conversion experience. Eventually I married a wonderful Catholic woman, but before long her knees gave out and they traded her to the Methodists. I keep telling her that as soon as she becomes a free agent, we can start going to church together again.

Even as an adult, my religious education continues. Recently my wife and I went on a retreat where we were supposed to ascertain our spiritual gifts. I was expecting a weekend full of soul searching, but instead they gave us a two-inch-thick fill-in-the-blank notebook. It was our SAT—Spiritual Aptitude Test: "Are you a leader in your church?" Since I help out with the parking every fourth Sunday, I checked "yes." "Do you open the Good Book

MY BIAS TOWARD THE PIOUS

regularly?" Well, every time one of the kids acts up, I quote an appropriate "Thou shalt not," so it was "yes" again. "Do you have the gift of celibacy?" I thought long and hard about that one and finally put down "I did, but I gave it back."

Anyone who isn't convinced that you can't laugh and have a strong faith at the same time should take another look at the Bible. It's filled with funny stuff. Like when God told Abraham (age one hundred) and Sarah (ninety) they were going to have a baby, they fell on their faces laughing. Abraham probably said, "Lord, can't we adopt?" But they had a son and named him Isaac, which means "laughter."

And what about Jonah? Most people think he was being punished when he was swallowed by the great fish. But he was out in the middle of the ocean and God had to get him to Ninevah. That whale wasn't punishment, it was transportation.

And when Jesus told the Jews not to cast their pearls before swine, he was communicating with humor, because Jews don't eat pork and didn't have any pigs. If we accept Jesus as a great teacher, it's hard not to believe he threw in a joke or two along the way.

So, as you work on the quizzes in this book, I hope you understand that we're simply trying to dispense some religious knowledge in the same entertaining way we do it every day on the Odyssey Channel. I promise you we'll never make fun of religion. In fact, when you're watching our TV show, if you ever hear me say, "So these two nuns walked into a bar . . ." you have my permission to switch back to *Wheel of Fortune*.

How to Play Inspiration, Please!

The *Inspiration, Please!* Trivia Quiz Book, based on the popular game seen coast to coast on the Odyssey Channel, allows you to play alone or with any number of friends. Each quiz includes fifteen questions, each with a follow-up bonus question on the same general subject, and an Inspiration Word puzzle.

IF YOU'RE PLAYING ALONE, simply write down your answers to the thirty questions in each quiz and check your answers. Then try to solve the Inspiration Word puzzle for that quiz (see page xviii).

IF TWO PEOPLE ARE PLAYING

1. One player reads each question and both players write down their answers. Check the answer page. Each player who answered correctly scores 5 points and gets to answer the bonus question, which is worth another 5 points.

2. Both players play the Inspiration Word puzzle (see page xviii), and the one with the highest total score wins.

HOW TO PLAY *INSPIRATION, PLEASE!*

IF MORE THAN TWO PEOPLE ARE PLAYING

1. For each quiz, players should alternate being the nonplaying "emcee," reading the questions, checking the answers, and keeping score.

2. After each question is read, the first player to call out a correct answer wins 5 points and a chance to answer the bonus question and score another 5 points. If the first person to answer is wrong, no points are deducted, but the other players are then allowed to call out an answer. Whoever guesses right wins the points and the chance at the bonus question.

3. All players play the Inspiration Word puzzle (see below), and the one with the highest total score wins.

HOW TO SOLVE THE INSPIRATION WORD PUZZLE

1. Each Inspiration Word is a common word whose meaning has some spiritual, inspirational, or religious connotation. Its diagram tells you how many letters are in the word.

2. The answer to each question in the Inspiration Round *begins* with one of the letters in the Inspiration Word, and the number in parentheses after each question tells you in which space to insert that letter. For example, if you're trying to guess this nine-letter Inspiration Word

___ ___ ___ ___ ___ ___ ___ ___ ___ ___
1   2   3   4   5   6   7   8   9   10

and the first question is Who was the third son of Adam and Eve? (6), the (6) tells you that the first letter of the correct answer (in this case "S" for Seth) belongs in space #6 in the Inspiration Word. As more letters are added to the diagram, the Inspiration Word become easier to identify.

How to Play *Inspiration, Please!*

3. If you're keeping score, each correct answer to an Inspiration Word question is worth 10 points, and the person who guesses the Inspiration Word wins an additional 50 points.

4. For each Inspiration Word, we've indicated how long it took a contestant on the TV show to guess that word, thereby allowing you to "play against the house."

>Good luck.
>And have fun.

The Inspiration, Please!
Trivia Quiz Book

Quiz #1

You Don't Have to Be Catholic...

1. What first name has been used by more popes than any other?

2. What is the Roman Catholic ceremony by which someone is declared a saint after his or her death?

3. A Catholic official whose duty is to argue against a proposed declaration of sainthood or blessedness is called what kind of advocate?

Your Answers

Bonus: When the College of Cardinals uses "scrutinies," are they eating, singing, or voting?

Bonus: Sainthood follows what ceremony by which a person is declared "blessed"?

Bonus: What is the title of a bishop of the highest rank?

Quiz #1

YOU DON'T HAVE TO BE CATHOLIC...

4. Two thirds of all Roman Catholic saints are of two nationalities. One is Italian. What is the other?

5. In the sixteenth century, the Ecumenical Council of the Catholic Church that met intermittently to define church doctrines and condemn the reformation was called the Council of . . . what?

6. What word describes a person's formal expulsion from the fellowship of the Catholic Church?

Your Answers

Bonus: Who was the first native-born American saint?

Bonus: That sixteenth-century council was named for the city in which it met. The city is in what country?

Bonus: In the Catholic Church, what word describes the relaxation of a particular law by a competent church authority?

— You Don't Have to Be Catholic... —

7. Following are three phrases, including one from the Bible. Each phrase has the same word missing. You fill in the missing word.

____ Time

Has the rain a ____?

____ of the Bride

8. The following headline might have appeared if there were tabloid newspapers in the year 1534. You identify the event the headline describes.

IGGY ORDERS NEW
ORDER FOR SOCIETY
FOLKS ONLY!

9. The following sentence contains the hidden name of several popes. You find the name.

WHERE'S THE
CLIP I USE?

_____
_____

_____
_____

_____
_____

Bonus:
Following are three more phrases, including one from the Bible, and each with the same word missing. You fill in the missing word.

The ____ King

Cowardly ____

What is stronger than a ____?

Bonus:
A member of this order is called a "scholastic" if he is preparing to become what?

Bonus:
The following sentence contains another hidden name of several popes. You find the name.

MY UNCLE
MENTIONED IT.

Quiz #1 — You Don't Have to Be Catholic...

10. Rearrange the letters in the word VANE to get the area of a church generally used only by the congregation.

11. The last rites of the Catholic Church are also known as extreme . . . what?

12. What is a priest most likely to do with an alb?

Your Answers

Bonus: Rearrange the letters in the word PEAS to get a recess in a church.

Bonus: Spiritual sanctification as a gift of the Holy Ghost is called Baptism of . . . what?

Bonus: If a bishop had a new miter, would he put it on his wall, on his Bible, or on his head?

You Don't Have to Be Catholic...

13. In 1928, Herbert Hoover became president of the United States by defeating the first Roman Catholic ever nominated for the office. Name him.

14. What is the largest Roman Catholic cathedral in the United States?

15. As founder of the Church of Rome, who is considered to have been the first pope?

_____

_____

_____

Bonus:
Nicholas Brekespeare was the only Englishman to be elected . . . what?

Bonus:
St. Patrick's Day is celebrated on March 17. Is that the day Saint Patrick was born, the day he became a saint, or the day he died?

Bonus:
The man who was born Angelo Roncalli took what name when he became pope in 1958?

Quiz #1

YOU DON'T HAVE TO BE CATHOLIC...

INSPIRATION WORD
(10 LETTERS)

YOUR ANSWERS

___ ___ ___ ___ ___ ___ ___ ___ ___ ___
 1   2   3   4   5   6   7   8   9   10

The correct answer to each question begins with one of the letters in the Inspiration Word, and the number in parentheses after the question tells you in which space (above) to insert that letter. Guess each answer and insert its first letter in the proper space. If your answers are right, you'll soon be able to identify the Inspiration Word.

On the *Inspiration, Please!* television show, this Inspiration Word was guessed after six letters.

1. What is the word for a memorial inscription on a tombstone? (5)
2. "I believe our heavenly father invented man because he was disappointed in the monkey." What creator of *Huckleberry Finn* said that? (7)
3. The first name of Miss Ferber, who wrote *Show Boat* and *Giant,* means "renewal" in Hebrew. What was her first name? (2)
4. What Christian denomination believes that God is one being, rejects the doctrine of the Trinity, and gives each congregation complete control over its affairs? (9)
5. According to the New Testament, in which of Jesus' discourses does he set forth the Golden Rule. (3)
6. What huge structures were built as royal tombs by the ancient Egyptians? (4)
7. One of the prominent civil rights organizations in the early days of the movement was the SCLC. What does the "L" stand for? (10)
8. Junipero Serra, the missionary who founded most of the Spanish missions in what is now California, was a member of what order? (8)
9. What famous poem concerning the sweetness of life and the pleasure of love was written by Omar Khayyám? (1)
10. In *Gone with the Wind,* what religion is the O'Hara family? (6)

ANSWERS TO QUIZ #1

YOU DON'T HAVE TO BE CATHOLIC...

1. John
2. Canonization
3. Devil's advocate
4. French
5. The Council of Trent
6. Excommunication
7. Father
8. Ignatius of Loyola founds the Society of Jesus or Jesuits.
9. Where's the cliP I USe? (Pius)
10. Nave
11. Extreme unction
12. He wears it. It's a long-sleeved vestment.
13. Al Smith
14. St. Patrick's Cathedral in New York City
15. Saint Peter

ANSWERS TO BONUS QUESTIONS:

1. Voting: Scrutinies are the ballots used to elect a pope.
2. Beatification
3. Archbishop
4. Elizabeth Seton
5. The city of Trent (Trento) is in Italy.
6. Dispensation
7. Lion
8. A priest
9. My unCLE MENTioned it. (Clement)
10. Apse
11. Baptism of fire or Baptism of the Holy Spirit or Baptism of the Holy Ghost
12. On his head. It's the official headdress of a bishop in the Western Church.
13. Pope. He became Adrian IV in 1154.
14. The day he died.
15. Pope John XXIII

INSPIRATION WORD ANSWERS

1. Epitaph
2. (Mark) Twain
3. Edna
4. Unitarian
5. The Sermon on the Mount
6. Pyramids
7. Leadership (The Southern Christian Leadership Conference)
8. Franciscan
9. *The Rubáiyát*
10. Catholic

And the Inspiration Word is:

1	2	3	4	5	6	7	8	9	10
R	E	S	P	E	C	T	F	U	L

Quiz #2

You Don't Have to Be Jewish...

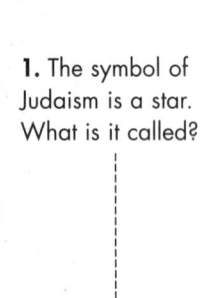

1. The symbol of Judaism is a star. What is it called?

2. According to the Jewish calendar, when does each new day begin?

3. On the Sabbath in a Jewish household, what does a menorah hold?

Your Answers

Bonus: How many points does the star have?

Bonus: The name of a foreign automobile is also a month of the Jewish calendar. Is it Nissan, Saab, or Audi?

Bonus: "Kol Nidre" is a prayer sung at the beginning of the service on what Jewish holy day?

8

You Don't Have to Be Jewish... — Quiz #2

4. Jewish congregations can be Orthodox, Conservative, or Reform. According to *The World Almanac*, in the United States are there more Orthodox, Conservative, or Reform congregations?

5. The year that Harry Truman defeated Thomas Dewey for president was the same year Israel achieved statehood. What year was it?

6. In observance of the commandment to cover the head in respect for God, a Jewish man wears a skullcap. What is it called?

Bonus: In the United States, which of the three branches of Judaism has the fewest number of congregations?

Bonus: In Israel, is "Hatikvah" the national flag, the national tree, or the national anthem?

Bonus: What does a Jewish man do with his "tallith" (pronounced TAH-liss)? Does he read from it, wear it, or eat it?

Quiz #2 — You Don't Have to Be Jewish...

7. Following are three phrases, including one from the Bible. Each phrase has the same word missing. You fill in the missing word.

____ and honey

Chocolate ____

____ of magnesia

8. The following headline might have appeared if there were tabloid newspapers in biblical times. You identify the event the headline describes.

MOE SPLITS BIG RED: CHARIOTEERS ALL WET!

9. The following sentence contains a hidden name from the Old Testament. You find the hidden name.

HE'LL SING A SOLO MONDAY.

Your Answers:

_____

_____

Bonus:
Following are three more phrases, including one from the Bible, and each with the same word missing. You fill in the missing word.

Ordinary ____

____ will talk

Let my ____ go

Bonus:
Moses is mentioned in the Bible more than seven hundred times. Only two men are mentioned more often, and Jesus is one of them. Who is the other?

Bonus:
The following sentence contains another hidden Old Testament name. You find the name.

I WISH MAE LAUGHED MORE.

10

You Don't Have to Be Jewish... — Quiz #2

10. Rearrange the letters in the word PAINS to get the name of one of the countries that Sephardic Jews come from.

11. For how many days do Jewish people celebrate the holiday of Chanukah?

12. A Jewish couple signs a "ketuba" in preparation for what?

Bonus:
Rearrange the letters in the word SHEAR to get the name of one of the twelve tribes of Israel.

Bonus:
On Chanukah, if you give a child a "dreidel," will he eat it, play with it, or put it in a cage?

Bonus:
A "minyan" is the minimum number of Jewish males at least thirteen years old required to be present for the lawful conduct of a public Jewish service. How many men constitute a "minyan"?

Quiz #2 — You Don't Have to Be Jewish...

13. At the end of a Jewish wedding ceremony, what does the groom traditionally step on and break?

14. When a rabbi mentions "Kaddish," is he or she referring to a food, a hat, or a prayer?

15. How many of Jesus' twelve disciples were born Jewish?

Your Answers

Bonus: The "chupah" is an important part of a traditional Jewish wedding ceremony. What is the "chupah"?

Bonus: Name the ram's horn that is sounded at synagogue services on certain Jewish holidays.

Bonus: In the Jewish religion, any person is considered a Jew if which of his parents is Jewish?

12

YOU DON'T HAVE TO BE JEWISH...

INSPIRATION WORD
(9 LETTERS)

YOUR ANSWERS

___ ___ ___ ___ ___ ___ ___ ___ ___
1   2   3   4   5   6   7   8   9

The correct answer to each question begins with one of the letters in the Inspiration Word, and the number in parentheses after the question tells you in which space (above) to insert that letter. Guess each answer and insert its first letter in the proper space. If your answers are right, you'll soon be able to identify the Inspiration Word.

On the *Inspiration, Please!* television show, this Inspiration Word was guessed after six letters.

1. Who is the Bible's most notorious female haircutter? (8)
2. What old-time movie cowboy got off his horse, Champion, long enough to make a hit record of "Rudolph the Red-Nosed Reindeer"? (3)
3. Job said, "I am escaped with the skin of my . . ." what? (6)
4. Name the prayer, at the beginning of a public ceremony, in which a clergyman calls for God's presence. (5)
5. In such books as *Adam Bede* and *Silas Marner*, Mary Ann Evans wrote about moral and social problems. Her pen name was George . . . what? (9)
6. In the sixteenth century, what was the religious movement that led to the establishment of the Protestant churches? (2)
7. Thanks to Natalie Wood and Edmund Gwenn, what New York City street is famous for a Christmas miracle? (4)
8. The unusual first name of the actress who won an Oscar nomination for *Pulp Fiction* is the same as a manifestation worshiped by some Hindus. What is the name? (7)
9. Who was slain in the Valley of Elah? (1)

ANSWERS TO QUIZ #2

YOU DON'T HAVE TO BE JEWISH...

1. Star of David
2. At sundown (or sunset)
3. Candles
4. Conservative
5. 1948
6. Yarmulke
7. Milk
8. Moses divides the Red Sea and his Egyptian enemies, in chariots, are drowned.
9. He'll sing a SOLO MONday. (Solomon)
10. Spain
11. Eight
12. Getting married. It's a marriage license.
13. A wineglass
14. A prayer. It's a prayer for mourners.
15. All twelve.

ANSWERS TO BONUS QUESTIONS:

1. Six
2. Nissan
3. Yom Kippur
4. Orthodox
5. The National Anthem
6. Wear it. It's a prayer shawl.
7. People
8. David
9. I wISH MAE Laughed more. (Ishmael)
10. Asher
11. Play with it. It's a toy, much like a top.
12. Ten
13. The canopy under which the bride and groom stand
14. Shofar
15. His mother

INSPIRATION WORD ANSWERS

1. Delilah
2. (Gene) Autry
3. Teeth
4. Invocation
5. (George) Eliot
6. Reformation
7. Thirty-fourth Street (The film is *Miracle on 34th Street*.)
8. Uma (Thurman)
9. Goliath

And the Inspiration Word is:

```
        9  8  7  6  5  4  3  2  1
        E  D  U  T  I  T  A  R  G
```

Quiz #3

You Don't Have to Be Protestant...

1. According to *The World Book Encyclopedia*, are more people in the United States affiliated with Episcopal churches, Methodist churches, or Presbyterian churches?

2. Roger Williams founded the first American church of what Protestant denomination?

3. To Seventh-day Adventists, what day of the week is the chief day of rest and religious observance?

Your Answers

_____
_____
_____

Bonus: According to a Gallup survey, what percentage of American adults have changed their religious denominational affiliation at least once: almost 1 percent, almost 10 percent, or almost 15 percent?

Bonus: Roger Williams founded what New England colony "in commemoration of God's providence"?

Bonus: A principal belief of Adventists is that something is imminent. What is it?

15

Quiz #3 — You Don't Have to Be Protestant...

4. John F. Kennedy's Catholic religion was well known. What was the Protestant denomination of his rival, Richard Nixon?

5. What is the official name of the Mormon Church?

6. Who said, "I look upon all the world as my Parish," and founded the Methodist Church in Great Britain and America?

Bonus: Although President Bill Clinton attended a Roman Catholic school for two years, he is a member of what Protestant denomination?

Bonus: After the Supreme Court ruled it illegal, the Mormon Church outlawed what practice pertaining to marriage?

Bonus: Charles, the brother of the founder of the Methodist Church in Great Britain and America, was famous for writing more than six thousand what?

You Don't Have to Be Protestant...

Quiz #3

7. Following are three phrases, including one from the Bible. Each phrase has the same word missing. You fill in the missing word.

Rain _____ from heaven

_____ pudding

Our daily _____

8. The following headline might have appeared if there were tabloid newspapers in the year 1517. You identify the event the headline describes.

MARTY POSTS 4 SCORE AND 15!

9. The following sentence contains the hidden name of a biblical place. You find the place.

I'LL BET HE LIKES STEAK.

Bonus: Following are three more phrases, including one from the Bible, and each with the same word missing. You fill in the missing word.

_____ degree burn

The _____ of all the fruit

_____ World War

Bonus: In 1521, "Marty" in the above headline was condemned as a heretic by what German council?

Bonus: The following sentence contains another hidden biblical place. You find the place.

I'M HOPING I LEAD THE BAND.

Quiz #3 — YOU DON'T HAVE TO BE PROTESTANT...

10. Rearrange the letters in the word NAME to get the last word in a prayer.

11. What evangelist, who was a spiritual counselor to several American presidents, wrote *Peace with God*, *Secrets of Happiness*, and *Angels*?

12. What Christian festival commemorates the descent of the Holy Ghost upon the apostles?

Your Answers

_____   _____   _____

Bonus:
Rearrange the letters in the word LIVED to get another word for Satan.

Bonus:
The evangelist conducted early work for the Youth for Christ crusade in the United States and what other country?

Bonus:
The same festival has another name beginning with "W." What is it?

18

You Don't Have to Be Protestant...

Quiz #3

13. Most preachers are good talkers. Name the Pentecostal preacher whose first name means "spoken."

14. *The Watchtower* is the magazine of what Christian religious group?

15. The Garden Grove Community Church in California, which pioneered drive-in churchgoing, is better known by what nickname?

Bonus: In what state will you find the university named for that preacher?

Bonus: Members of that religious group consider one of Adam's sons as the first member of their society. Which son?

Bonus: What founder of the church is also a best-selling author?

Quiz #3

— You Don't Have to Be Protestant... —

INSPIRATION WORD
(8 LETTERS)

Your Answers

___ ___ ___ ___ ___ ___ ___ ___
 1   2   3   4   5   6   7   8

The correct answer to each question begins with one of the letters in the Inspiration Word, and the number in parentheses after the question tells you in which space (above) to insert that letter. Guess each answer, and insert its first letter in the proper space. If your answers are right, you'll soon be able to identify the Inspiration Word.

On the *Inspiration, Please!* television show, this Inspiration Word was guessed after seven letters.

1. At a wedding in a church or synagogue, who escorts you to your seat? (3)
2. "By and by, Lord, by and by," says an old gospel song that asks "Will the circle be . . ." what? (7)
3. If it's been blessed by a priest, what kind of water is it? (5)
4. The American Society of what international organization was founded by Clara Barton? (2)
5. Who is credited with writing the two books of the Bible addressed to Theophilus? (8)
6. Mardi Gras is also known as Shrove . . . what? (4)
7. According to the gospels, Jesus went to pick some fruit and then cursed the tree and made it wither. What kind of tree was it? (6)
8. After a religious experience, Isabella Hardenburgh, a former slave, changed her name to Sojourner . . . what? (1)

Answers to Quiz #3

You Don't Have to Be Protestant...

1. Methodist
2. Baptist
3. Saturday
4. Quaker or Society of Friends
5. The Church of Jesus Christ of Latter-day Saints
6. John Wesley
7. Bread
8. Martin Luther posts his ninety-five theses.
9. I'll BET HE Likes steak. (Bethel)
10. Amen
11. Billy Graham
12. Pentecost
13. Oral Roberts
14. Jehovah's Witnesses
15. The Crystal Cathedral

Answers to Bonus Questions:

1. Almost 15 percent
2. Rhode Island Colony
3. The Second Coming of Christ
4. Baptist
5. Polygamy
6. Hymns
7. First
8. The Diet of Worms
9. I'm hopinG I LEAD the band. (Gilead)
10. Devil
11. England
12. Whitsunday
13. Oklahoma (It's in Tulsa.)
14. Abel
15. Robert Schuller

Inspiration Word Answers

1. Usher
2. Unbroken
3. Holy water
4. The Red Cross
5. Luke
6. Shrove Tuesday
7. Fig
8. Truth

And the Inspiration Word is:

1	2	3	4	5	6	7	8
T	R	U	T	H	F	U	L

Quiz #4

Eastern Standard

1. What is the official religion of Egypt?

2. What is the title of the worldly leader of Tibetan Buddhists?

3. Amritsar, in India, is the holy city of what religion?

YOUR ANSWERS

Bonus:
Fewer than 10 percent of present-day Egyptians belong to what ancient Egyptian Christian Church?

Bonus:
A six-year-old boy is said to be the reincarnation of the second most important monk in Tibetan Buddhism. What is that monk called?

Bonus:
When members of that religion talk about the "granth," are they referring to their leader, their holy book, or their temple?

EASTERN STANDARD — Quiz #4

4. In what religion is the supreme and absolute power called Brahman?

5. The meditation techniques taught by Maharishi Mahesh Yogi are called "T.M." What does T.M. stand for?

6. In a Muslim mosque, the mihrab, or prayer niche, always points toward what city?

Bonus: Members of that religion worship several gods whom they consider reflections of Brahman. How many of these gods are there?

Bonus: According to Chinese philosophy and religion, what are the two "Y" words that stand for the two principles whose interaction influences destiny?

Bonus: What is the name of the tall tower of a mosque from which worshipers are called to prayer?

Quiz #4 — EASTERN STANDARD

7. Following are three phrases, including one from the Bible. Each phrase has the same word missing. You fill in the missing word.

_____ lode

The _____ of all living

_____ Teresa

8. The following headline might have appeared in a tabloid newspaper in 1947. You identify the story the headline describes.

FREE AT LAST! JINNAH IS MUSLIMS' LEADER OF THE "PAK"

9. The following sentence contains a hidden river that is sacred to Hindus. Find the river.

WATCH RONALD REAGAN GESTURE.

Your Answers

_____

_____

_____

Bonus:
Following are three more phrases, including one from the Bible, and each with the same word missing. You fill in the missing word.

_____ am I

Slap _____

_____ go lucky

Bonus:
In Urdu, one of its official languages, does the name of the country referred to in the above headline mean "land of the sun," "land of the pure," or "land of the free"?

Bonus:
The following sentence contains a hidden language of the Middle East. Find the language.

I HEAR A BICYCLE HORN.

24

Eastern Standard — Quiz #4

10. Rearrange the letters is the word PLANE to get the Asian country that is second only to India in the size of its Hindu population.

11. What is the sacred text of Islam?

12. What Hindu religious leader, when asked his religion, said, "I am a Hindu. I am a Muslim. I am a Christian. I am a Buddhist. I am a Jew"?

Bonus: Rearrange the letters in the word MAIDEN to get the Saudi Arabian city where the tomb of Muhammad is located.

Bonus: In the Islam religion, who is the only god?

Bonus: What word, which in English means "great soul," was applied to that Hindu leader as a title of respect?

Quiz #4 — EASTERN STANDARD

13. Zen is a sect of what religion?

14. What country has the world's largest Buddhist population?

15. What religion, which teaches the essential worth of all religions, the unity of all races, and the equality of the sexes, has its United States headquarters in Wilmette, Illinois?

Your Answers

Bonus:
Zen was founded in the sixth century in what country?

Bonus:
Jakarta is the capital of the country with the world's largest Muslim population? Name the country.

Bonus:
Was that religion founded in China, Japan, or Iran?

26

EASTERN STANDARD

INSPIRATION WORD
(9 LETTERS)

YOUR ANSWERS

___ ___ ___ ___ ___ ___ ___ ___ ___
 1   2   3   4   5   6   7   8   9

The correct answer to each question begins with one of the letters in the Inspiration Word, and the number in parentheses after the question tells you in which space (above) to insert that letter. Guess each answer, and insert its first letter in the proper space. If your answers are right, you'll soon be able to identify the Inspiration Word.

On the *Inspiration, Please!* television show, this Inspiration Word was guessed after only three letters, which was a show record.

1. The apostle Paul was the mentor of what young pastor for whom two books of the New Testament are named? (2)
2. What university in Philadelphia sounds like a house of worship? (9)
3. What is the first book of the Old Testament to record the giving of the Ten Commandments to Moses? (5)
4. "The Bible is no mere book, but a living creature, with a power that conquers all that oppose it." Those are the words of what emperor of France? (4)
5. What Christian festival falls on January 6 and is sometimes known as the Feast of the Magi? (7)
6. Complete this quote from Isaiah: "Watchman, what of the _____?" (8)
7. Name the food that was miraculously provided to the Israelites in the wilderness. (6)
8. What word that means "the service of the Mass, exclusive of the canon," also means "commonplace"? (3)
9. What Old Testament character is considered the founder of the ancient Hebrew nation? (1)

ANSWERS TO QUIZ #4

EASTERN STANDARD

1. Islam
2. The Dalai Lama
3. Sikhism
4. Hinduism
5. Transcendental Meditation
6. Mecca
7. Mother
8. Pakistan gains independence and Mohammed Ali Jinnah is its first governor-general.
9. Watch Ronald ReaGAN GESture. (Ganges)
10. Nepal
11. The Koran
12. Mohandas K. Gandhi
13. Buddhism
14. Japan
15. Baha'i

ANSWERS TO BONUS QUESTIONS:

1. The Coptic Church
2. The Panchen Lama
3. Their holy book
4. Three
5. Yin and Yang
6. Minaret
7. Happy
8. Land of the Pure
9. I heAR A BICycle horn. (Arabic)
10. Medina
11. Allah
12. Mahatma
13. China
14. Indonesia
15. Iran

INSPIRATION WORD ANSWERS

1. Timothy
2. Temple
3. Exodus
4. Napoleon
5. Epiphany
6. Night
7. Manna
8. Ordinary
9. Abraham

And the Inspiration Word is:

1	2	3	4	5	6	7	8	9
A	T	O	N	E	M	E	N	T

Quiz #5

Quid Pro Quote

1. "Those who labor in the earth are the chosen people of God." Those words were written by the third president of the United States. Name him.

2. "The only guide to a man is his conscience." Those words were spoken by what British prime minister?

3. "I am neither an atheist nor a rationalist. I believe in God, and am of the religion of my father." Those are the words of what French general who was known as "The Little Corporal"?

Bonus: "That book is the rock on which our republic rests." That description of the Bible was made by the U.S. president known as "Old Hickory." Name him.

Bonus: "Conscience is but a word that cowards use." Who wrote those words in his play *Richard the Third*?

Bonus: "All service ranks the same with God." Those are the words of what poet who married Elizabeth Barrett?

QUIZ #5 — QUID PRO QUOTE

4. In "The Ballad of Reading Gaol," what British author wrote, "How else but through a broken heart may Lord Christ enter in"?

5. According to the book of Exodus, to keep it holy, what day should you remember?

6. "As a well-spent day brings happy sleep, so life well-used brings happy death." Those words were written by the man who painted *Mona Lisa*. Name him.

Your Answers

_____   _____   _____
_____   _____   _____

Bonus: "The only religious way to think of death is as part and parcel of life." What German-born novelist wrote that line in *The Magic Mountain*?

Bonus: Also according to the book of Exodus, "The Lord is my strength and song, and he is become my . . ." what?

Bonus: "All I have seen teaches me to trust the creator for all I have not seen." Those are the words of what American essayist and poet who wrote "Days," which many consider his greatest poem.

QUID PRO QUOTE — Quiz #5

7. Following are three phrases, including one from the Bible. Each phrase has the same word missing. You fill in the missing word.

One language and few ____

____ and music

A war of ____

8. The following headline might have appeared if there were tabloid newspapers in the year 1611. You identify the event the headline describes.

JIM'S NEW BOOK DEBUTS; LOOKS LIKE BEST-SELLER!

9. The following sentence contains the hidden name of a Biblical character. You find the name.

LULU KEEPS QUOTING ME.

Bonus:
Following are three more phrases, including one from the Bible, and each with the same word missing. You fill in the missing word.

Don't forget to ____ a check

____ them upon the doorposts

Bonus:
Three quarters of a century before the headlined event took place, Miles Coverdale's Bible was published. Why was it noteworthy?

Bonus:
The following sentence contains another hidden name of a Biblical character. You find the name.

QUOTING CELEBRITIES IS A HABIT.

Quiz #5 — Quid Pro Quote

10. Rearrange the letters in the word MILKER to get the name of the poet who said, "Only God can make a tree."

11. According to the old saying, the road to hell is paved with . . . what?

12. After his inauguration in 1789, what president said, "Almighty God, we make our earnest prayer that thou will keep the United States in thy holy protection"?

Your Answers

_____ _____ _____

Bonus: Rearrange the letters in the word SKATE to get the name of the English poet who said, "Behold the clear religion of heaven."

Bonus: According to the saying based on William Congreve, "Hell hath no fury like . . ." what?

Bonus: "Where annual elections end, there slavery begins." Those are the words of the second president of the United States. Name him.

32

Quid Pro Quote

13. Name the author who wrote these lines in *Pudd'nhead Wilson's Calendar:* "Adam was but human. This explains it all. He did not want the apple for the apple's sake. He wanted it only because it was forbidden."

14. "The Kingdom of God is within you." What author of *War and Peace* wrote those words?

15. According to the book of Psalms, "Out of the mouths of babes and sucklings" what has God ordained?

Bonus:
In the book *Winesburg, Ohio*, you'll find this line: "Everyone in the world is Christ and they are all crucified." Who wrote it?

Bonus:
"Prosperity is the blessing of the Old Testament. Adversity is the blessing of the New." Those words were written by the essayist and philosopher who some people suspect wrote Shakespeare's plays. Name him.

Bonus:
Here's another quote from the book of Psalms. You fill in the blank. "Make a ____ noise unto the Lord, all ye lands."

33

Quiz #5

QUID PRO QUOTE

INSPIRATION WORD
(8 LETTERS)

Your Answers

___ ___ ___ ___ ___ ___ ___ ___
 1   2   3   4   5   6   7   8

The correct answer to each question begins with one of the letters in the Inspiration Word, and the number in parentheses after the question tells you in which space (above) to insert that letter. Guess each answer, and insert its first letter in the proper space. If your answers are right, you'll soon be able to identify the Inspiration Word.

On the *Inspiration, Please!* television show, this Inspiration Word was guessed after seven letters.

1. The Greek word for Thanksgiving is another name for the sacrament of Holy Communion. What is the word? (5)
2. In celebration of Easter, the early Mesopotamians were the first people to color them. What are they? (2)
3. What poet, whose works include "Ash Wednesday" and "Journey of the Magi," also wrote the play *Murder in the Cathedral*? (7)
4. Yes, Virginia, there is a Santa Claus. It's a town about thirty miles from Evansville in what midwestern state? (4)
5. What was the first bird sent out from Noah's ark? (8)
6. What country music singer is famous for his album called *Joshua Judges Ruth*, but even more famous for his brief marriage to Julia Roberts? (3)
7. Joseph had his share of troubles with his brothers. What was the name of his youngest brother? (1)
8. Joseph's father, Jacob, was tricked into marrying Leah when her father covered her face with . . . what? (6)

Answers to Quiz #5

Quid Pro Quote

1. Thomas Jefferson
2. Winston Churchill
3. Napoleon Bonaparte
4. Oscar Wilde
5. The sabbath
6. Leonardo da Vinci
7. Words
8. Publication of the King James version of the Bible
9. LuLU KEeps quoting me. (Luke)
10. (Joyce) Kilmer
11. Good intentions
12. George Washington
13. Mark Twain
14. Leo Tolstoy
15. Strength

Answers to Bonus Questions:

1. Andrew Jackson
2. William Shakespeare
3. Robert Browning
4. Thomas Mann
5. Salvation
6. Ralph Waldo Emerson
7. Write
8. It was the first complete Bible in English.
9. Quoting celebrities is A HABit. (Ahab)
10. (John) Keats
11. A woman scorned
12. John Adams
13. Sherwood Anderson
14. Sir Francis Bacon
15. Joyful

Inspiration Word Answers

1. Eucharist
2. Eggs
3. (T. S.) Eliot
4. Indiana
5. Raven
6. (Lyle) Lovett
7. Benjamin
8. A veil

And the Inspiration Word is:

1	2	3	4	5	6	7	8
B	E	L	I	E	V	E	R

Quiz #6

Old Testamentality

1. What are God's first words in the Old Testament?

2. If there were a telephone directory listing all of the Old Testament characters alphabetically, who would be listed first?

3. Which book of the Old Testament means "beginning"?

Bonus: God's words on the temple wall—"Mene, mene, tekel, upharsin"—were interpreted by Daniel as foretelling the destruction of whose kingdom?

Bonus: Alphabetically speaking, which is the first of Noah's three sons?

Bonus: Which book of the Old Testament means "repetition of the law"?

OLD TESTAMENTALITY — QUIZ #6

4. Which of Adam's sons built the first city?

5. How long was Jonah inside the great fish?

6. As a sign that God would cause the walls of the city to tumble, who marched around Jericho seven times?

_____   _____   _____

Bonus:
The son who built the first city named it after *his* son. What was its name?

Bonus:
To what great city did the Lord send Jonah to warn the people to give up their evil ways?

Bonus:
The blast of what musical instruments, played by the Israelites, caused Jericho's walls to fall?

Quiz #6 — OLD TESTAMENTALITY

7. Following are three phrases, including one from the Bible. Each phrase has the same word missing. You fill in the missing word.

____ tell

____ for your servants

Let us ____

8. The following headline might have appeared if there were tabloid newspapers in approximately 1,000 B.C. You identify the event the headline describes.

BIG GUY GETS STONED! DAVID SAYS "I DID IT"

9. The following sentence contains the hidden name of an Old Testament character. You find the name.

AN EMIR I AM NOT.

Your Answers

_____   _____   _____
_____   _____   _____

Bonus:
Following are three more phrases, including one from the Bible, and each with the same word missing. You fill in the missing word.

A strong ____ against the enemy

Ivory ____

____ of Babel

Bonus:
Name the son of King Saul who was one of David's best friends.

Bonus:
The following sentence contains the hidden name of another Old Testament character. You find the name.

I'M NEAR A CHELSEA PUB.

Old Testamentality — Quiz #6

10. Rearrange the letters in the word NAILED to get the name of an Old Testament character.

11. Only one book of the Old Testament begins with the letter "R." Which book?

12. If you decide to read the Old Testament cover to cover, will you read nineteen books, twenty-nine books, or thirty-nine books?

_____ _____ _____
_____ _____ _____

Bonus:
Rearrange the letters in the word HUMAN to get the name of another Old Testament character.

Bonus:
The names of two Old Testament books begin with the letter "P." Name one of them.

Bonus:
Does the Old Testament have more or fewer books than the New Testament?

Quiz #9 — OLD TESTAMENTALITY

13. Today, what Old Testament book could have been called "Wapner and Ito"?

14. After the flood, on what mountain did Noah's ark come to rest?

15. If Esau and Jacob were around today and played professional baseball, which American league team would they be most likely to join?

Your Answers:

_____   _____   _____
_____   _____   _____

Bonus: What Old Testament book provided the title for the Leon Uris novel and Paul Newman movie about the early years of the State of Israel?

Bonus: In what country is that mountain located?

Bonus: Rebecca was the mother of Esau and Jacob. Who was their father?

40

OLD TESTAMENTALITY

INSPIRATION WORD
(9 LETTERS)

___ ___ ___ ___ ___ ___ ___ ___ ___
1 **2** **3** **4** **5** **6** **7** **8** **9**

The correct answer to each question begins with one of the letters in the Inspiration Word, and the number in parentheses after the question tells you in which space (above) to insert that letter. Guess each answer, and insert its first letter in the proper space. If your answers are right, you'll soon be able to identify the Inspiration Word.

On the *Inspiration, Please!* television show, this Inspiration Word was guessed after eight letters.

1. Two epic poems by Homer have inspired readers for almost three thousand years. One of them is *The Iliad*. Name the other. (5)

2. What word that's been eliminated from many wedding ceremonies used to follow the words "love" and "honor"? (3)

3. What prophet walked around naked and barefoot for three years? (7)

4. Memphis, now most familiar to us as a city in Tennessee, was once the name of the capital of what ancient country? (9)

5. What word describes a person who denies or disbelieves the existence of God? (1)

6. The Book of Psalms refers to what Mount in the far north as "The city of the great King"? (8)

7. The moral "One good turn deserves another" applies to the old story about Androcles, who removed a thorn from the foot of what animal? (4)

8. The song "Sit Down, You're Rockin' the Boat" includes the line, "And the Devil will drag you under by the sharp lapel of your checkered coat." It's from what Broadway musical? (6)

9. In 1682, calling it a "holy experiment," who established the state of Pennsylvania? (2)

Answers to Quiz #6

Old Testamentality

1. "Let there be light."
2. Aaron
3. Genesis
4. Cain
5. Three days and three nights
6. Joshua
7. Pray
8. David slays Goliath with one shot from his slingshot.
9. An eMIR I AM not. (Miriam)
10. Daniel
11. Ruth
12. 39
13. Judges (Judge Wapner was on the TV show called *People's Court,* and Judge Ito presided over the O. J. Simpson trial.)
14. Mount Ararat
15. The Minnesota Twins (Esau and Jacob were twins.)

Answers to Bonus Questions:

1. Belshazzar (The words mean "Numbered, numbered, weighed, divided.")
2. Ham (His two brothers, in alphabetical order, were Japheth and Shem.)
3. Deuteronomy
4. Enoch
5. Nineveh
6. Trumpets
7. Tower
8. Jonathan
9. I'm neaR A CHELesa pub. (Rachel)
10. Nahum
11. Psalms and proverbs
12. More. The New Testament consists of twenty-seven books.
13. Exodus
14. Turkey
15. Isaac

Inspiration Word Answers

1. *(The) Odyssey*
2. Obey
3. Isaiah
4. Egypt
5. Atheist
6. Zion
7. Lion
8. *Guys and Dolls*
9. (William) Penn

And the Inspiration Word is:

1	2	3	4	5	6	7	8	9
A	P	O	L	O	G	I	Z	E

Quiz #7

NEW TESTAMENTALITY

1. What is the first book of the New Testament that is *not* named for a person?

2. The first part of the book contains a message to the churches and the second part contains a series of visions of the future. What New Testament book is it?

3. According to the New Testament, which animal opens the seventh seal?

Your Answers

_____   _____   _____
_____   _____   _____

Bonus:
What is the last book of the New Testament that *is* named for a person?

Bonus:
That same New Testament book is thought to have been written by which apostle while he was in exile on the Isle of Patmos?

Bonus:
When the seventh seal is opened, what is heard?

Quiz #7 — New Testamentality

4. The Epistle to the Galatians refers to "fruits of the spirit." Name the one that starts with the letter "J."

5. According to the New Testament, the root of all evil is the love of . . . what?

6. According to the Book of Revelation, the new heavenly city will have twelve of them, each made from a large pearl. What are they?

Your Answers

_____   _____   _____

Bonus: Two of the fruits of the spirit start with the letter "P." Name one of them.

Bonus: According to the New Testament, what shall cover the multitude of sins?

Bonus: The Book of Revelation mentions the size of the new heavenly city. Will it be 15 square miles, 150 square miles or 1,500 square miles?

New Testamentality

7. Following are three phrases, including one from the New Testament. Each phrase has the same word missing. You fill in the missing word.

An evil _____

Do not quench the _____

That's the _____

___

8. The following headline might have appeared if there were tabloid newspapers in biblical times. You identify the New Testament event it describes.

THIS MARVEL IS A FIRST: H₂O BECOMES SAUTERNES!

___

9. The following sentence contains the hidden name of a character from the New Testament. You find the hidden name.

IN A BAR ABBA SINGS.

___

Bonus:
Following are three more phrases, including one from the New Testament, and each with the same word missing. You fill in the missing word.

The dividing _____ of hostility

The Berlin _____

_____-eyed pike

Bonus:
In the "marvel" described in the above headline, were there one, three, or six stone jars involved?

Bonus:
The following sentence contains the hidden name of another New Testament character. You find the hidden name.

NOTE HER ODD WAYS.

Quiz #7: NEW TESTAMENTALITY

10. Rearrange the letters in the name LYDIA to get how often, according to the Book of Acts, the churches increased in number.

11. Complete this quote from the Gospel of Matthew: "Whosoever shall smite thee on thy right ____, turn to him the other also."

12. Complete this quote from the Gospel of Mark: "For many bear false ____ against him."

Your Answers:

_____

_____

_____

Bonus: Rearrange the letters in the word VALES to get the person who, according to Luke, was dear to a centurion.

Bonus: Complete this quote from the Gospel of Matthew: "What therefore God hath joined together, let no man put ____."

Bonus: Complete this quote from the Gospel of Mark: "Suffer the little ____ to come unto me and forbid them not."

New Testamentality — Quiz #7

13. Complete this quote from the Gospel of Luke: "Father, _____ them, for they know not what they do."

14. Complete this quote from the Gospel of John: "The truth shall make you _____."

15. The Book of Thessalonians tells of a time when believers in Christ will be caught up in the clouds and meet the Lord. What is this event commonly called?

Bonus: Complete this quote from the Gospel of Luke: "Do this in _____ of me."

Bonus: Complete this quote from the Gospel of John: "Greater love hath no man than this, that a man lay down his life for his _____."

Bonus: Before this event occurs, is the Lord himself supposed to descend from Heaven with a shout, a spear, or a shield?

47

Quiz #7

NEW TESTAMENTALITY

INSPIRATION WORD
(9 LETTERS)

YOUR ANSWERS

___ ___ ___ ___ ___ ___ ___ ___ ___
 1   2   3   4   5   6   7   8   9

The correct answer to each question begins with one of the letters in the Inspiration Word, and the number in parentheses after the question tells you in which space (above) to insert that letter. Guess each answer and insert its first letter in the proper space. If your answers are right, you'll soon be able to identify the Inspiration Word.

On the *Inspiration, Please!* television show, this Inspiration Word was guessed after seven letters.

1. "Emir" is a Muslim title of nobility. A country governed by an emir is called what? (4)
2. Although many of his religious paintings were done in Spain, the Spanish name by which he's known means "The Greek." Who was he? (6)
3. In their worship services, members of what religion read from a book called *Science and Health*? (8)
4. The holy wars called the Crusades began in what century? (2)
5. The rebirth of the soul in a new body after death is called . . . what? (5)
6. Name the son of Cain who became the father of Methuselah. (9)
7. Fill in the blank in the name of this film in which Tom Skerritt played a Presbyterian minister: *A _____ Runs Through It*. (1)
8. What is the title of a permanent diplomatic representative of the pope? (7)
9. In "The Battle Hymn of the Republic," what is the Lord "trampling out . . . where the grapes of wrath are stored"? (3)

ANSWERS TO QUIZ #7

NEW TESTAMENTALITY

1. Acts
2. Revelation
3. A lamb
4. Joy
5. Money
6. Gates
7. Spirit
8. In his first miracle, Jesus turned water into wine.
9. In a BAR ABBA Sings. (Barabbas)
10. Daily
11. Cheek
12. Witness
13. Forgive
14. Free
15. The Rapture

ANSWERS TO BONUS QUESTIONS:

1. Jude
2. John
3. Nothing; silence
4. Peace and patience
5. Charity
6. 1,500
7. Wall
8. Six. Jesus turned six stone jars of water into wine.
9. Note HER ODd ways. (Herod)
10. Slave
11. Asunder
12. Children
13. Remembrance
14. Friends
15. A shout

INSPIRATION WORD ANSWERS

1. Emirate
2. El Greco
3. Christian Scientists
4. Eleventh
5. Reincarnation
6. Enoch
7. River
8. Nuncio
9. Vintage

And the Inspiration Word is:

R E V E R E N C E
1 2 3 4 5 6 7 8 9

Quiz #8

Drawing a Blank

1. Fill in the blank in this line from the Book of Genesis: "Be fruitful and ____."

2. Fill in the blank in this line from Matthew: "No man can serve two ____."

3. Fill in the blank in the title of this hymn: "Glorious Things of Thee Are ____."

Your Answers

_____   _____   _____

Bonus: Here's another line from Genesis. You fill in the blank. "And Adam called his wife's name Eve, because she was the ____ of all living."

Bonus: Here's another quote from Matthew. You fill in the blank. "Ye have sown much and bring in ____."

Bonus: Fill in the blank in this title of another famous hymn: "Lead, Kindly ____."

DRAWING A BLANK — Quiz #8

4. Fill in the blank in this quote from the Book of Acts: "Almost thou persuadest me to be a ____."

5. Jesus invited him who is without sin to cast the first . . . what?

6. Fill in the blank in this line from the 23rd Psalm: "Thou preparest a ____ before me in the presence of mine enemies."

Bonus: Here's another quote from the Book of Acts. Fill in the blank. "Much learning doth make thee ____."

Bonus: According to Saint Paul, the wages of sin is . . . what?

Bonus: Here's another line from the 23rd Psalm. You fill in the blank. "And I will ____ in the house of the Lord forever."

51

Quiz #8 — DRAWING A BLANK

7. Following are three phrases, including one from the Bible. Each phrase has the same word missing. You fill in the missing word.

Oh, ____

A ____ is born for adversity

____-in-law

8. The following headline might have appeared if there were tabloid newspapers in biblical times. You identify the event the headline describes.

FOUR WRITERS MAKE FOUR G'S; MARK IS THE FIRST

9. The following sentence contains the hidden name of a mythological god. You find the hidden name.

BLANKS DON'T FAZE US.

Your Answers

_____

_____

Bonus:
Following are three more phrases, including one from the Bible, and each with the same word missing. You fill in the missing word.

The sins of my ____

____ hostel

Reckless____

Bonus:
Of the four "G's" in the headline above, which is the shortest?

Bonus:
The following sentence contains the hidden name of an Old Testament character. You find the name.

DON'T ERASE THESE BLANKS.

52

DRAWING A BLANK — Quiz #8

10. Rearrange the letters in the word BEARD to get the word that completes this quote from John: "I am the ____ of life."

11. Here's a well-known line from the Gospel of John. You fill in the blank. "Ask, and ye shall ____."

12. Here's a quote from the Apocrypha. You fill in the blank. "Let us now praise famous ____."

Bonus: Rearrange the letters in the word TEAM to get what Matthew said "Ye gave me when I was hungered."

Bonus: Here's another quote from John. You fill in the blank. "Do not judge by ____."

Bonus: Here's another line from the Apocrypha. You fill in the blank. "Speech finely framed delighteth the ____."

53

Quiz #8 — DRAWING A BLANK

13. According to John Wesley, what is "indeed next to godliness"?

14. Here's a line from the Gospel of Luke. You fill in the blank. "____, heal thyself."

15. This line is from the Book of Psalms. You fill in the blank. "My God, my God, why has thou ____ me?"

Your Answers:

_____
_____
_____

Bonus: The Book of Psalms refers to "He that hath clean hands and a pure . . . what?"

Bonus: Here's another quote from Luke. You fill in the blank. "The poor and the maimed and the halt and the ____."

Bonus: Here's another line from the Book of Psalms. You fill in the blank. "Thy word is a ____ unto my feet, and a light unto my path."

54

DRAWING A BLANK

INSPIRATION WORD
(8 LETTERS)

___ ___ ___ ___ ___ ___ ___ ___
 1   2   3   4   5   6   7   8

The correct answer to each question begins with one of the letters in the Inspiration Word, and the number in parentheses after the question tells you in which space (above) to insert that letter. Guess each answer, and insert its first letter in the proper space. If your answers are right, you'll soon be able to identify the Inspiration Word.

On the *Inspiration, Please!* television show, this Inspiration Word was guessed after six letters.

1. The captain in *Moby Dick* has the same name as the biblical Jezebel's husband. What is the name? (4)
2. If you kiss the Blarney Stone, you'll become adept in the art of flattery, according to the legend of what country? (6)
3. Adam's sin in disobeying God in the Garden of Eden is known as *what* sin? (2)
4. The geyser known as Old Faithful is in what national park? (8)
5. In 1946, what former first lady was elected chairperson of the United Nations Human Rights Commission? (3)
6. In the seventeenth century, the last of the great religious wars of Europe is identified by how many years it lasted. How many years was it? (7)
7. In the 1960s, which of the Beatles said, "We're more popular than Jesus now"? (5)
8. King Louis XIV of France had to exert his influence on the Church to get a religious burial for what author of *Tartuffe* and *The School for Wives*? (1)

Answers to Quiz #8

Drawing a Blank

1. Multiply
2. Masters
3. Spoken
4. Christian
5. Stone
6. Table
7. Brother
8. Matthew, Mark, Luke, and John write the Gospels. Mark is the first.
9. Blanks don't faZE US. (Zeus)
10. Bread
11. Receive
12. Men
13. Cleanliness
14. Physician
15. Forsaken

Answers to Bonus Questions:

1. Mother
2. Little
3. Light
4. Mad
5. Death
6. Dwell
7. Youth
8. The Gospel of Mark
9. Don't eraSE THese blanks. (Seth)
10. Meat
11. Appearance
12. Ears
13. Heart
14. Blind
15. Lamp

Inspiration Word Answers

1. Ahab
2. Ireland
3. Original sin
4. Yellowstone
5. (Eleanor) Roosevelt
6. Thirty (It was called The Thirty Years' War.)
7. (John) Lennon
8. Molière

And the Inspiration Word is:

1	2	3	4	5	6	7	8
M	O	R	A	L	I	T	Y

Quiz #9

That's Entertainment

1. What late comedian, born Nathan Birnbaum, played the title role in the movie *Oh God*?

2. What legendary Broadway comedy by Clarence Day ends when the irascible patriarch of a Victorian family shouts, "I'm going to be baptized, damn it!"

3. The characters in what Shakespeare play include Friar Lawrence and Friar John?

Bonus:
What comic actor and director, born Allen Stewart Konigsberg, said, "I don't want to achieve immortality through my work. I want to achieve it through not dying"?

Bonus:
In what Thornton Wilder play does a minister address a letter to "Grover's Corners, Sutton County, New Hampshire, United States of America, Continent of North America, Western Hemisphere, The Earth, The Solar System, The Universe, The Mind of God"?

Bonus:
The characters in what Shakespeare play include a priest, a ghost, and Rosencrantz and Guildenstern?

Quiz #9 — THAT'S ENTERTAINMENT

4. Name the Oscar-winning film about two Olympic runners, one of whom refuses to run on Sunday because of his religious beliefs.

5. In what Broadway musical does a baseball fan make a pact with the devil?

6. They weren't exactly heavenly, but Kate Jackson, Cheryl Ladd, and Jaclyn Smith starred on what heavenly sounding television series?

YOUR ANSWERS

_____   _____   _____

Bonus:
Why should that film make you think of the prophet Elijah?

Bonus:
In that same musical, a quartet of baseball players sings "You gotta have . . ." what?

Bonus:
Elizabeth Montgomery was called TV's prettiest witch in what comedy series?

58

That's Entertainment

7. Following are three phrases, including one from the Bible. Each phrase has the same word missing. You fill in the missing word.

___ *Boat*

___ me thy glory

___ and tell

8. The following headline might have appeared if there were tabloid newspapers in about 6 B.C. You identify the event the headline describes.

WISE GUYS CO-STAR IN *THREE MEN AND A BABY*

9. The following sentence contains the hidden title of the movie that featured the song "Thank Heaven for Little Girls." You find the film title.

THE MAGI GIVE GIFTS.

Bonus:
Following are three more phrases, including one from the Bible, and each with the same word missing. You fill in the missing word.

___ your age

___ of mercy

Time for the Lord to ___

Bonus:
The "wise guys" in the above headline came from what direction?

Bonus:
The following sentence contains the hidden last name of the actor who starred in a controversial film called *King David* several years before he starred in *An Officer and a Gentleman*. You find his name.

HIS RAGE RETURNED.

59

Quiz #9 — That's Entertainment

10. Rearrange the letters in the word RESISTS to get the title of the Swoosie Kurtz TV series that sounds like it's about nuns.

11. In what film was Linda Blair so possessed by the devil that it made her head spin?

12. In what musical film does a nun sing "Climb Every Mountain"?

Bonus:
Rearrange the letters in the word STRIPE to get the Oscar-winning role Bing Crosby played in *Going My Way*.

Bonus:
What male comic created a character named Geraldine who always said, "The Devil made me do it"?

Bonus:
In the same musical film, a trainee nun becomes the governess to the children of an Austrian widower. What is the family name?

That's Entertainment

13. Name the televangelist couple who ran afoul of the law while producing their TV shows on the P.T.L. network.

14. In a film that won the Academy Award for best picture, what title character saved Jews from the death camps by putting them to work in his factory?

15. Name the film in which Audrey Hepburn plays a young Belgian woman who joins a strict religious order and eventually returns to ordinary life.

Bonus:
In the early days of television, what American bishop delivered weekly sermons on a program called *Life Is Worth Living*?

Bonus:
Robby Benson, Maximilian Schell, and Rod Steiger starred in what film about a family feud between Zionists and Hasidic Jews that sours a friendship between two boys?

Bonus:
In the film called *The Inn of the Sixth Happiness*, what actress played a missionary in war-torn China.

Quiz #9

THAT'S ENTERTAINMENT

INSPIRATION WORD
(10 LETTERS)

Your Answers

___ ___ ___ ___ ___ ___ ___ ___ ___ ___
 1   2   3   4   5   6   7   8   9   10

The correct answer to each question begins with one of the letters in the Inspiration Word, and the number in parentheses after the question tells you in which space (above) to insert that letter. Guess each answer, and insert its first letter in the proper space. If your answers are right, you'll soon be able to identify the Inspiration Word.

On the *Inspiration, Please!* television show, this Inspiration Word was guessed after eight letters.

1. King Darius had *whom* put into the lions' den?(6)
2. Ministers and nobles became servants of what "terrible" Russian tsar? (3)
3. What dance is often used to tell stories of the gods in Hawaii? (8)
4. Osiris, King of the Dead, was worshiped in what ancient country? (4)
5. What word describes a painting of a sacred person that is itself regarded as sacred? (9)
6. What Southern Baptist minister founded the Moral Majority? (1)
7. In what country is the sacred city of Mecca? (7)
8. In the Bible, whose preaching caused a boy to fall asleep and then fall out of a window? (10)
9. In one of his plays, Jean-Paul Sartre wrote, "Hell is other people." Name the play. (5)
10. Richard Burton played a centurion who oversaw Jesus' crucifixion in a film whose title was an article of clothing. What article was it? (2)

Answers to Quiz #9

That's Entertainment

1. George Burns
2. Life with Father
3. Romeo and Juliet
4. Chariots of Fire
5. Damn Yankees
6. Charlie's Angels
7. Show
8. The three Wise Men bring gifts to the newborn Jesus.
9. The MaGI GIve gifts. (Gigi)
10. Sisters
11. The Exorcist
12. The Sound of Music
13. Jim and Tammy Faye Bakker
14. Oscar Schindler (The film is Schindler's List.)
15. The Nun's Story

Answers to Bonus Questions:

1. Woody Allen
2. Our Town
3. Hamlet
4. When a chariot of fire appeared, Elijah went up to heaven in a whirlwind.
5. Heart
6. Bewitched
7. Act
8. East
9. His raGE REturned. ([Richard] Gere)
10. Priest
11. Flip Wilson
12. Trapp or von Trapp
13. Bishop Fulton J. Sheen
14. The Chosen
15. Ingrid Bergman

Inspiration Word Answers

1. Daniel
2. Ivan
3. The hula
4. Egypt
5. Icon
6. (Jerry) Falwell
7. Saudi Arabia
8. Paul
9. No Exit
10. A robe. The film was The Robe.

And the Inspiration Word is:

```
  1  2  3  4  5  6  7  8  9  10
  F  R  I  E  N  D  S  H  I  P
```

Quiz #10

Animal Crackers

1. What animal is also the name of a formal papal document?

2. Samson ate honey out of the carcass of what animal?

3. What is the state bird in seven states *and* a high ecclesiastic appointed by the pope?

Your Answers

Bonus:
According to Exodus, Moses was to tell Pharaoh that if he did not "Let my people go," his country would be plagued by what amphibians?

Bonus:
John the Baptist also had some strange eating habits. According to the Bible, did he eat worms, snakes, or locusts?

Bonus:
Spelled one way, it's a horse's easy gallop. Spelled another way, it's the religious official of a synagogue who sings or chants prayers. What is it?

ANIMAL CRACKERS

Quiz # 10

4. According to legend, what Christian saint once slew a fire-breathing dragon?

5. What animal is mentioned in the Bible more often than any other?

6. On his triumphant entry into Jerusalem, what kind of animal did Jesus ride?

Bonus: That dragon killer is the patron saint of two European countries. Name one of them.

Bonus: According to Ecclesiastes, what living animal is better than a dead lion?

Bonus: That same animal protested to what prophet that it had seen an angel?

Quiz #10 — ANIMAL CRACKERS

7. Following are three phrases, including one from the Bible. Each phrase has the same word missing. You fill in the missing word.

A pale _____

_____ and buggy

A _____ of another color

8. The following headline might have appeared if there were tabloid newspapers in biblical times. You identify the event the headline describes.

M.I.A. RETURNS! DAD PREPARES MEAL BUT KID SAYS "TOO FAT"

9. The following sentence contains the hidden name of an animal mentioned in the Bible. You find the animal.

YOU'LL DO VERY WELL.

Your Answers:

_____

_____

Bonus:
Following are three more phrases, including one from the Bible, and each with the same word missing. You fill in the missing word.

Leg of _____

_____ chops

A _____ as his offering

Bonus:
At the event described in the headline, what relative didn't feel like partying?

Bonus:
The following sentence contains the hidden name of another animal mentioned in the Bible. You find the animal.

IS THAT FOUNTAIN THE TREVI PERHAPS?

66

ANIMAL CRACKERS

Quiz #10

10. Rearrange the letters in the word SABER to get two animals that mauled the children for laughing at Elisha.

11. What animal did God provide as a substitute for the sacrifice of Isaac?

12. The animal used to describe a person or organization that is exempt from criticism is a sacred . . . what?

Bonus: Rearrange the letters in the word REPENTS to get the snake that in the Bible is called the Devil.

Bonus: What animal did God send to destroy the plant that had provided shade for Jonah?

Bonus: What river that's mentioned in the Bible sounds like a female jungle cat?

Quiz #10 — ANIMAL CRACKERS

13. An elected official who advocates war or a belligerent national attitude is called what kind of bird?

14. Christmas Day, December 25, falls under the Zodiac sign represented by the goat. What sign is it?

15. Ganesh, the Hindu God of Wisdom, is always represented with the head of what animal?

Bonus: According to Jesus, what kind of birds could be sold two for a farthing?

Bonus: Depending on the date on which it occurs, Easter can fall under one of two signs of the Zodiac, represented by the ram and the bull. Name one of the two signs.

Bonus: Today you'll find this bird on the menu of expensive restaurants. But it was food for the Israelites in the wilderness. What bird is it?

ANIMAL CRACKERS

INSPIRATION WORD
(9 LETTERS)

YOUR ANSWERS

___ ___ ___ ___ ___ ___ ___ ___ ___
 1   2   3   4   5   6   7   8   9

The correct answer to each question begins with one of the letters in the Inspiration Word, and the number in parentheses after the question tells you in which space (above) to insert that letter. Guess each answer, and insert its first letter in the proper space. If your answers are right, you'll soon be able to identify the Inspiration Word.

On the *Inspiration, Please!* television show, this Inspiration Word was guessed after eight letters.

1. Especially at Easter time, what flower is the symbol of purity? (3)
2. Who sold his birthright to his brother? (9)
3. What TV sitcom star played the leading role in the film *The Santa Clause*? (6)
4. The Hebrew word for "my master" is the word for what Jewish spiritual leader? (5)
5. In what film does a child named Damien appear to be diabolically inspired? (2)
6. Wilma Mankiller, the first female chief of her tribal nation, was committed to preserving her tribe's spirituality. What tribe? (8)
7. The English king who founded Westminster Abbey was known as "The Confessor." What was his first name? (4)
8. A devotion that consists of prayers or services on nine consecutive days is called . . . what? (7)
9. What French statesman, before he was known for his diplomatic achievements under Napoleon the First, and at the Congress of Vienna, was a priest? (1)

Answers to Quiz #10

Animal Crackers

1. Bull
2. Lion
3. Cardinal
4. Saint George
5. Sheep (200 times)
6. A donkey
7. Horse
8. The prodigal son returns home. His father cooks the "fatted calf."
9. You'll DO VEry well. (Dove)
10. Bears
11. A ram
12. Cow
13. Hawk
14. Capricorn
15. Elephant

Answers to Bonus Questions:

1. Frogs
2. Locusts
3. Canter/Cantor
4. England and Portugal
5. A dog
6. Baalam
7. Lamb
8. The prodigal son's brother
9. Is that fountain the TreVI PERhaps? (Viper)
10. Serpent
11. A worm
12. Tigris (tigress)
13. Sparrows
14. Aries (Ram) or Taurus (Bull)
15. Quail

Inspiration Word Answers

1. Lily
2. Esau (He sold it to Jacob.)
3. Tim Allen
4. Rabbi
5. *The Omen*
6. Cherokee
7. Edward (He was known as Saint Edward, the Confessor.)
8. Novena
9. Talleyrand or Talleyrand-Périgord (His full name was Charles-Maurice de Talleyrand-Périgord, Prince de Bénévent!)

And the Inspiration Word is:

1	2	3	4	5	6	7	8	9
T	O	L	E	R	A	N	C	E

Quiz #11

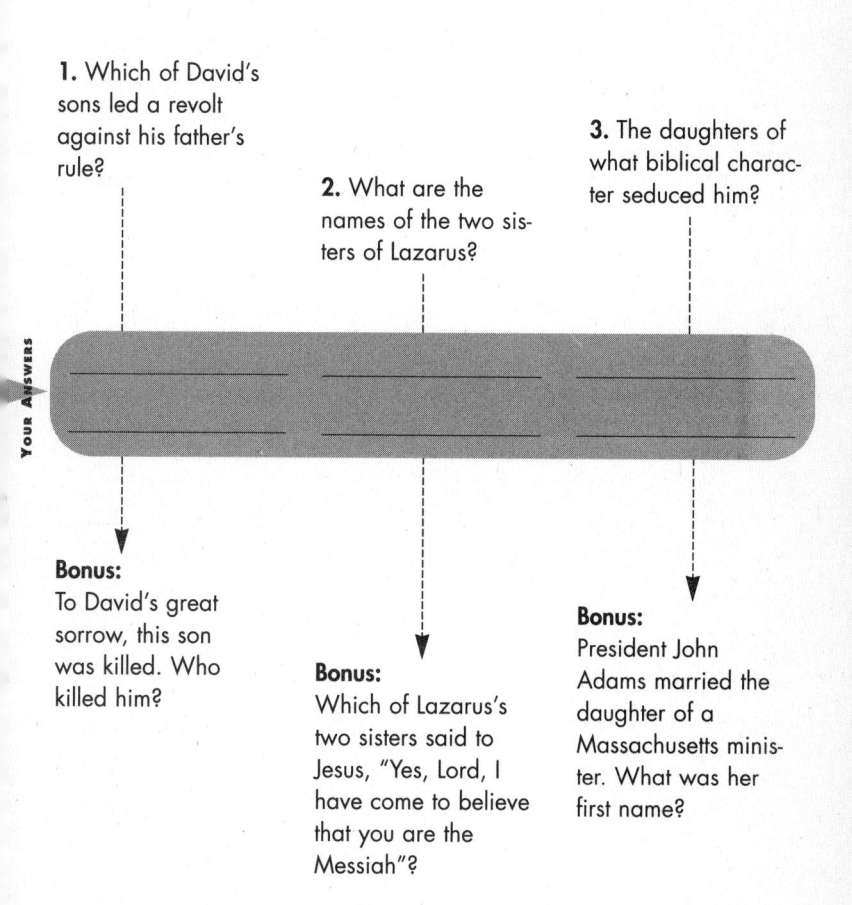

It's All Relative

1. Which of David's sons led a revolt against his father's rule?

2. What are the names of the two sisters of Lazarus?

3. The daughters of what biblical character seduced him?

Bonus: To David's great sorrow, this son was killed. Who killed him?

Bonus: Which of Lazarus's two sisters said to Jesus, "Yes, Lord, I have come to believe that you are the Messiah"?

Bonus: President John Adams married the daughter of a Massachusetts minister. What was her first name?

Quiz #11 — It's All Relative

4. How was Methuselah related to Noah?

5. How are Ishmael and Hagar related?

6. Who was the mother of John the Baptist?

Your Answers:

_____   _____   _____
_____   _____   _____

Bonus: Methuselah was renowned as the oldest man who ever lived. According to the Bible, how old was he when he died?

Bonus: According to the book of Genesis, Ishmael and Hagar are cast out of whose family?

Bonus: Who was the father of John the Baptist?

IT'S ALL RELATIVE

7. Following are three phrases, including one from the Bible. Each phrase has the same word missing. You fill in the missing word.

____ Nature

____ Goose

A ____ of nations

8. The following headline might have appeared if there were tabloid newspapers in biblical times. You identify the event the headline describes.

JOE'S DAD IS A SEW-AND-SEW, SO KID GETS FANCY THREADS!

9. The following sentence contains the hidden name of the biblical wife of Boaz. You find the hidden name.

I'M IN A RUT HERE.

Bonus:
Following are three more phrases, including one from the Bible, and each with the same word missing. You fill in the missing word.

The ____ of the Regiment

Turn back, my ____

Yes, my darling ____

Bonus:
The "dad" referred to in the above headline had many sons. How many?

Bonus:
The following sentence contains the hidden name of the biblical wife of Ahasuerus. You find the hidden name.

I SEE TREES THERE.

Quiz #11 — It's All Relative

10. Rearrange the letters in the word OMANI to get the name of a famous biblical mother-in-law.

11. Fill in the blank in this title of a well-known hymn: "Faith of Our ____."

12. You'll find the name of what biblical stepfather on packages of a popular brand of children's aspirin.

Bonus:
Rearrange the letters in the word BANAL to get the name of Rebecca's brother.

Bonus:
The above-mentioned hymn includes a line about "living still" in spite of three tribulations. Name one of them.

Bonus:
What Old Testament king had seven hundred wives (in addition to three hundred concubines)?

It's All Relative — Quiz #11

13. What famous biblical character was the husband of Zipporah?

14. In the Bible, she's the daughter of Jacob and Leah. In a popular folk song, someone's in the kitchen with her. What's her name?

15. The name of what singing brothers of the 1960s makes them sound good, honest, and virtuous?

Bonus: Who was Zipporah's father?

Bonus: In the Bible, he's the cousin of King Saul. In the comic strip, it's the first name of Mr. Yokum of Dogpatch. What's his name?

Bonus: King David was the youngest of how many brothers?

IT'S ALL RELATIVE

INSPIRATION WORD
(10 LETTERS)

___ ___ ___ ___ ___ ___ ___ ___ ___ ___
 1   2   3   4   5   6   7   8   9   10

The correct answer to each question begins with one of the letters in the Inspiration Word, and the number in parentheses after the question tells you in which space (above) to insert that letter. Guess each answer and insert its first letter in the proper space. If your answers are right, you'll soon be able to identify the Inspiration Word.

On the *Inspiration, Please!* television show, this Inspiration Word was guessed after only four letters.

1. What is the third book of the Old Testament? (4)
2. After a long search for her lover, the title character in the narrative poem *Evangeline*, becomes a Sister of Charity. Who wrote *Evangeline*? (6)
3. Who is the leader of the Palestine Liberation Organization? (9)
4. According to the book of Revelation, where is the place where the final battle will be fought between the forces of good and evil? (2)
5. Three of the first five American presidents were of the same Protestant denomination. What denomination is it? (5)
6. What city is the capital of Israel? (8)
7. If you're in a state of intense happiness, you're said to be in seventh . . . what? (1)
8. In the days before the Civil War, the system by which Harriet Tubman helped slaves escape to the north was called what kind of railroad? (7)
9. Who is the third person of the Trinity? (10)
10. The name of what rebellious archangel, identified with Satan, also is the planet Venus when it appears as the morning star? (3)

Answers to Quiz #11

It's All Relative

1. Absalom
2. Mary and Martha
3. Lot
4. He was Noah's grandfather.
5. Hagar was Ishmael's mother.
6. Elisabeth
7. Mother
8. Jacob sews Joseph a coat of many colors.
9. I'm in a RUT Here. (Ruth)
10. Naomi
11. "Faith of Our Fathers"
12. Saint Joseph
13. Moses
14. Dinah
15. The Righteous Brothers

Answers to Bonus Questions:

1. Joab
2. Martha
3. Abigail
4. 969 years
5. Abraham
6. Zacharias or Zachariah
7. Daughter
8. Twelve
9. I see treES THERe. (Esther)
10. Laban
11. Dungeon, fire, and sword
12. Solomon
13. Jethro
14. Abner
15. Eight

Inspiration Word Answers

1. Leviticus
2. (Henry Wadsworth) Longfellow
3. (Yasir) Arafat
4. Armageddon
5. Episcopal (The first three Episcopal presidents were Washington, Madison, and Monroe.)
6. Jerusalem
7. Heaven
8. Underground
9. Holy Ghost or Holy Spirit
10. Lucifer

And the Inspiration Word is:

1	2	3	4	5	6	7	8	9	10
H	A	L	L	E	L	U	J	A	H

Quiz #12

Hit or Myth

1. Name the mountain that, according to mythology, was the home of the Greek gods.

2. What was the life-giving drink of the mythological gods?

3. What planet is named for the mythological Roman god of war?

Your Answers

Bonus: Who was the king of the ancient Greek gods?

Bonus: The food or perfume of the gods was called what?

Bonus: The twin sons of the Roman god of war were the legendary founders of Rome. What were their names?

HIT OR MYTH — Quiz #12

4. Name one of the two days of the week that is *not* named for a Norse god or goddess.

5. What mythological character, who had to support the world on his shoulder, shares his name with a book of maps?

6. Poseidon was the ancient Greek god of the sea. With whom was he identified by the Romans?

_____

_____

_____

Bonus:
The Roman goddess of the moon is also the goddess of hunting and the protectress of women. Who is she?

Bonus:
In Greek mythology, Jason and the Argonauts set out to find the wool of a sacred animal. What was this treasure called?

Bonus:
To the ancient Romans, Cupid was the god of love. With whom was he identified by the Greeks?

Quiz #12 — Hit or Myth

7. Following are three phrases, including one from the Bible. Each phrase has the same word missing. You fill in the missing word

Bacchus, Roman god of ____

And ____ to gladden the heart

Days of ____ and Roses

8. The following headline might have appeared if the mythological gods had tabloid newspapers. You identify the story the headline describes.

EVIL WOMAN'S CURIOSITY FORCES HER TO OPEN CRATE

9. The following sentence contains the hidden name of a mythological character. Find the character.

HE FRAMED US ALL.

Your Answers

_____

_____

_____

Bonus:
Following are three more phrases, including one from the Bible, and each with the same word missing. You fill in the missing word.

Kronos, Greek god of ____

____ of judgment

____ on my hands

Bonus:
In addition to other things, the crate referred to in the headline contained "man's last comfort." What was it?

Bonus:
The following sentence contains the name of another mythological character. Find the character.

SET THE RAT TRAPS.

HIT OR MYTH — Quiz #12

10. Rearrange the letters in the word TONERS to get the oldest and wisest of the Greeks in the Trojan War.

11. The wife of the Roman god Jupiter was called "Queen of Heaven." What was her name?

12. The title of what 1995 Woody Allen film includes the name of the Greek goddess of love and beauty?

_____   _____   _____

Bonus:
Rearrange the letters in the word STAVE to get the name of the Roman goddess of the hearth.

Bonus:
What is the name of a mythological character who has one eye in the center of his forehead?

Bonus:
The name of what manufacturer of sneakers also is the name of the Greek goddess of victory?

Quiz #12 — Hit or Myth

13. According to Greek mythology, who is the handsome youth who admired himself so much that he fell in love with his own reflection?

14. What Greek god of the forests and meadows, half man and half goat, played pipes made out of reeds?

15. What name is shared by a god of the underworld, a planet, and a Walt Disney cartoon character?

Your Answers

Bonus: The Greek goddess Athena tamed what winged horse?

Bonus: Who was the nymph who loved the handsome youth, but was so hurt by his coldness that she faded away except for her voice?

Bonus: Both the Greeks and Romans had the same name for the god of, among other things, light, healing, and manly beauty. Name him.

HIT OR MYTH — Quiz #12

INSPIRATION WORD
(9 LETTERS)

YOUR ANSWERS

___ ___ ___ ___ ___ ___ ___ ___ ___
 1   2   3   4   5   6   7   8   9

The correct answer to each question begins with one of the letters in the Inspiration Word, and the number in parentheses after the question tells you in which space (above) to insert that letter. Guess each answer, and insert its first letter in the proper space. If your answers are right, you'll soon be able to identify the Inspiration Word.

On the *Inspiration, Please!* television show, this Inspiration Word was guessed after seven letters.

1. What word spelled one way means "unemployed," and spelled another way means "a material object that is worshiped as a deity"? (5)
2. During the O. J. Simpson trial, bodyguards for Simpson's lawyer Johnnie Cochran were supplied by the black religious and civil rights organization called the Nation of . . . what? (3)
3. Jacob had four wives, one daughter, and how many sons? (6)
4. In biblical times, it's what grew on the heads of Raphael and Michael. Today it's a very thin pasta. What is it? (8)
5. The John Bunyan novel that is considered one of the world's great religious classics is called *Pilgrim's* . . . what? (2)
6. The song that says "We're going to the chapel, and we're gonna get married" is called "The Chapel of . . ." what? (9)
7. According to superstition, you'll have bad luck if you open what outdoor device indoors? (7)
8. Name the Israeli prime minister who was assassinated in 1995. (4)
9. What is the name of the room in a church in which sacred vestments are kept? (1)

Answers to Quiz #12

Hit or Myth

1. Mount Olympus
2. Nectar
3. Mars
4. Sunday and Monday (named for the sun and the moon)
5. Atlas
6. Neptune
7. Wine
8. Pandora opens the box containing all of the world's evils and sins.
9. He fraMED US All (Medusa)
10. Nestor
11. Juno
12. *Mighty Aphrodite*
13. Narcissus
14. Pan
15. Pluto

Answers to Bonus Questions:

1. Zeus
2. Ambrosia
3. Romulus and Remus
4. Diana
5. The golden fleece
6. Eros
7. Time
8. Hope
9. Set tHE RAt traps. (Hera)
10. Vesta
11. Cyclops
12. Nike
13. Echo
14. Pegasus
15. Apollo

Inspiration Word Answers

1. Idle/Idol
2. Islam
3. Twelve
4. Angel hair
5. *Progress*
6. Love
7. Umbrella
8. (Yitzhak) Rabin
9. Sacristy

And the Inspiration Word is:

1	2	3	4	5	6	7	8	9
S	P	I	R	I	T	U	A	L

Quiz #13

Food for Thought

1. Observant Jews and Muslims don't eat pork. What meat do observant Hindus avoid?

2. Here's a quote from Deuteronomy. Complete it with the name of a food: "Man doth not live by *what* alone."

3. How many men, not counting women and children, did Jesus feed with five loaves of bread and two fish?

Bonus: Members of most traditional Hindu castes eat only with the right hand. Is it because they consider the left hand unsteady, unholy, or unclean?

Bonus: Here's another quote from Deuteronomy. Complete it with the name of another food: "He kept him as the *what* of his eye."

Bonus: After the people had their fill, how many basketsful of food were left over?

Quiz #13 — FOOD FOR THOUGHT

4. In about A.D. 610, when a monk who was baking folded some dough in the shape of a child's arms in prayer, what snack food was born?

5. A huge wine bottle that holds six and a half quarts has the same name as what biblical old-timer?

6. For what kind of food did Esau sell his birthright?

Bonus: According to Isaiah, a cake made of what fruit should be applied to a boil so that the victim might recover?

Bonus: A champagne bottle that holds four fifths of a gallon has the same name as what two kings of ancient Israel?

Bonus: What did Elisha miraculously eliminate from stew?

Food for Thought

7. Following are three phrases, including one from the Bible. Each phrase has the same word missing. You fill in the missing word.

Sour _____

Gather the fallen _____

The _____ of Wrath

8. Following is a headline that might have appeared if there were tabloid newspapers in biblical times. You identify the event the headline describes.

AARON MAKES 24-CARAT VEAL, BUT MO COMES HOME AND DESTROYS IT!

9. The following sentence contains the name of the meal to which, according to Luke, you should not invite your friends.

THERE'S NO GOOD IN NERVOUSNESS.

Bonus:
Following are three more phrases, including one from the Bible, and each with the same word missing. You fill in the missing word.

_____ to the Lord

_____ or famine

_____ your eyes

Bonus:
How were Aaron and Moses related?

Bonus:
The following sentence contains the name of the meal that Martha served Jesus in Bethany.

I MESS UP PERIODICALLY.

Quiz #13 — Food for Thought

10. Rearrange the letters in the word LAST to get the seasoning that Lot had plenty of.

11. According to the Book of Proverbs, what food drips from the lips of a loose woman?

12. According to the song "The Twelve Days of Christmas," on the eighth day I gave my love eight maids. What were they doing?

Your Answers

Bonus:
Rearrange the letters in the word WINES to get one of the animals the Lord told Moses the people must not eat because it is unclean.

Bonus:
In biblical times, the robes of the high priests were decorated with pictures of a tropical fruit that was thought to symbolize fertility. What fruit was it?

Bonus:
According to the old song, Good King Wenceslas looked out on the feast of . . . whom?

Food for Thought

Quiz #13

13. On what holiday do Jews serve a meal called a Seder?

14. What kind of cake would biblical characters like Gabriel be most likely to enjoy?

15. What kind of artichoke is named for an ancient holy city?

Bonus: What unleavened bread is served at a Seder?

Bonus: What biblical sheepherder has the same name as a contemporary maker of chocolate chip cookies?

Bonus: Spelled one way it's a biblical kingdom. Spelled another way it's a Dutch cheese. What is it?

89

Quiz #13

FOOD FOR THOUGHT

INSPIRATION WORD
(9 LETTERS)

YOUR ANSWERS

___ ___ ___ ___ ___ ___ ___ ___ ___
 1   2   3   4   5   6   7   8   9

The correct answer to each question begins with one of the letters in the Inspiration Word, and the number in parentheses after the question tells you in which space (above) to insert that letter. Guess each answer, and insert its first letter in the proper space. If your answers are right, you'll soon be able to identify the Inspiration Word.

On the *Inspiration, Please!* television show, this Inspiration Word was guessed after only four letters.

1. According to the Book of Leviticus, it was punishable by death, and one of the Ten Commandments says, "Thou shalt not commit it." What is it? (7)
2. Fill in the blank in the title of this Gospel musical: "Your ____ Too Short to Box with God." (2)
3. What New Testament book immediately follows I and II Timothy and, like them, is an epistle named for a disciple and companion of Paul? (5)
4. The first plague in Egypt brought about by Moses was the turning to blood the waters of what river? (3)
5. What was the name of the pharaoh who finally set the Hebrew slaves free? (8)
6. What North American country has the world's largest Christian population? (6)
7. Name the time of merrymaking that immediately precedes Lent and comes from an old Italian word that means, literally, "taking meat away." (4)
8. What Jewish holy day is the Day of Atonement? (9)
9. What breed of dog gets its name from the monks who used them to rescue lost travelers? (1)

Answers to Quiz #13

Food for Thought

1. Beef
2. Bread
3. Five thousand
4. The pretzel
5. Methuselah
6. Pottage or stew
7. Grapes
8. Aaron creates a golden calf; Moses returns from Sinai and destroys it.
9. There's no gooD IN NERvousness. (Dinner)
10. Salt
11. Honey
12. Milking or a-milking
13. Passover
14. Angel food cake (Gabriel was, of course, an angel.)
15. Jerusalem artichoke

Answers to Bonus Questions:

1. Unclean
2. Apple
3. Twelve
4. Figs
5. Jeroboam
6. Poison
7. Feast
8. They were brothers.
9. I mesS UP PERiodically. (Supper)
10. Swine
11. Pomegranate
12. Stephen
13. Matzo
14. Amos (The cookie maker is known as "Famous Amos.")
15. Edom/Edam

Inspiration Word Answers

1. Adultery
2. Arms
3. Titus
4. The Nile
5. Ramses
6. The United States
7. Carnival
8. Yom Kippur
9. St. Bernard

And the Inspiration Word is:

S	A	N	C	T	U	A	R	Y
1	2	3	4	5	6	7	8	9

Quiz #14

Book Review

1. *East of Eden*, a book loosely based on the book of Genesis, was written by what American novelist?

2. The best-selling Morris West novel about a Russian pope is called *The Shoes of the . . .* what?

3. The literary classic called *The Canterbury Tales* is about a group of people on a pilgrimage to a shrine in Canterbury. Who wrote it?

Bonus: What American author wrote *Absalom, Absalom!*, *Requiem for a Nun*, and *A Fable*, in which the experiences of a soldier symbolize the Passion of Christ?

Bonus: The title of the Morris West novel refers to what biblical character?

Bonus: The pilgrims in *The Canterbury Tales* are on their way to visit the shrine of what murdered archbishop?

BOOK REVIEW — Quiz #14

4. What Victor Hugo novel, which became a successful Broadway musical, was banned by the Catholic Church when it was published in 1862?

5. The hymn that includes the words "Lord God of hosts, be with us yet, lest we forget, lest we forget" was written by what author of *Gunga Din*?

6. What twentieth-century president of the United States wrote a book called *Profiles in Courage*?

Bonus: The Catholic Church banned the works of the man who wrote *The Count of Monte Cristo,* and his son, who wrote *Camille.* What was their last name?

Bonus: What daughter of missionary parents wrote *The Good Earth*?

Bonus: What twentieth-century president of the United States wrote a book called *The Blood of Abraham*?

Quiz #14 — BOOK REVIEW

7. Following are three phrases, including one from the Bible. Each phrase has the same word missing. You fill in the missing word.

_____ worm

One for the _____

A _____ of remembrance

Bonus:
Following are three more phrases, including one from the Bible, and each with the same word missing. You fill in the missing word.

_____ assassination

The unchangeable _____ of his purpose

_____ study

8. Following is a headline that might have appeared if there were tabloid newspapers in the year 1843. You identify the event the headline describes.

CHUCK WRITES GHOST STORY AND MAKES "EB" A YULE FOOL!

Bonus:
At the end of the "ghost story" in the above headline, a child speaks a memorable five-word line. What are the five words?

9. The following sentence contains the hidden last name of the English romantic poet who wrote "The Eve of St. Agnes." You find the hidden name.

LET JACK EAT SUPPER.

Bonus:
The following sentence contains the hidden last name of the author of *The Agony and the Ecstasy*, about the friction between Pope Julius II and Michelangelo. You find the hidden name.

I'LL EAT JUST ONE BITE.

94

Book Review

Quiz #14

10. Rearrange the letters in the word CATS to get a book of the New Testament.

11. What great poet of the Middle Ages wrote of Hell and Paradise in his allegorical poem, *The Divine Comedy*?

12. What American author of *In Cold Blood* also wrote *Answered Prayers*?

_____   _____   _____
_____   _____   _____

Bonus:
Rearrange the letters in the word THREES to get a book of the Old Testament.

Bonus:
The woman who is the guide in *The Divine Comedy* was the love of the author's life. What was her name?

Bonus:
"When the gods wish to punish us, they answer our prayers." Those words were written by what author of *The Importance of Being Earnest*?

Quiz #14 — Book Review

13. Name the fictional Himalayan heaven-on-earth in James Hilton's novel *Lost Horizon*.

14. What twelve-book epic, based on the biblical story of the creation, was written by English poet John Milton?

15. It's a book in Heaven listing everyone who has eternal life, and according to Revelation, anyone will be thrown into the lake of fire if his name is not found in the book. What is it called?

Your Answers

Bonus: In Samuel Coleridge's poem, in what Eden-like place did Kubla Khan "a stately pleasure-dome decree"?

Bonus: While writing that epic, and its sequel, John Milton suffered from what physical handicap?

Bonus: "I'll be asking God to stretch a hand to you in the hour of death." Who wrote those words in *The Playboy of the Western World*?

BOOK REVIEW

QUIZ #14

INSPIRATION WORD
(9 LETTERS)

YOUR ANSWERS

___ ___ ___ ___ ___ ___ ___ ___ ___
 1   2   3   4   5   6   7   8   9

The correct answer to each question begins with one of the letters in the Inspiration Word, and the number in parentheses after the question tells you in which space (above) to insert that letter. Guess each answer, and insert its first letter in the proper space. If your answers are right, you'll soon be able to identify the Inspiration Word.

On the *Inspiration, Please!* television show, this Inspiration Word was guessed after eight letters.

1. The hospital in which it took place was called St. Elegius, but the television series was called *St. . . .* what? (9)
2. The film *Ben Hur* was subtitled *A Tale of the Christ*. Who won a best actor Oscar for his role in the film? (2)
3. When Paul and Silas were in prison, what force of nature loosened their chains? (5)
4. All Hallows' Eve is celebrated in what month? (7)
5. The first three words in the song "God Bless America" are "God Bless America." What is the fourth word? (4)
6. Who did Samuel select to be the first king of the Israelites? (6)
7. What American poet, who wrote *Leaves of Grass*, once described grass as "the handkerchief of the Lord"? (1)
8. The hero who recaptured Jerusalem from the Syrians and rededicated the temple was Judas . . . who? (8)
9. Which branch of Judaism insists on retaining traditional Jewish laws and customs as they relate to liturgy, diet, and dress? (3)

Answers to Quiz #14

Book Review

1. John Steinbeck
2. Fisherman
3. Geoffrey Chaucer
4. *Les Misérables*
5. Rudyard Kipling
6. John F. Kennedy
7. Book
8. Charles Dickens writes *A Christmas Carol* about Ebenezer Scrooge.
9. Let JacK EAT Supper. ([John] Keats)
10. Acts
11. Dante (Dante Alighieri)
12. Truman Capote
13. Shangri-La
14. *Paradise Lost*
15. The Book of Life

Answers to Bonus Questions:

1. William Faulkner
2. Peter
3. Saint Thomas à Becket
4. Dumas (Alexandre Dumas père, the father; and Alexandre Dumas fils, the son)
5. Pearl Buck
6. Jimmy Carter
7. Character
8. "God bless us every one" is pronounced by Tiny Tim.
9. I'll eat juST ONE bite. ([Irving] Stone)
10. Esther
11. Beatrice
12. Oscar Wilde
13. Xanadu
14. He was blind.
15. John Millington Synge

Inspiration Word Answers

1. Elsewhere
2. (Charlton) Heston
3. Earthquake
4. October (It's Halloween.)
5. Land ("Land that I love")
6. Saul
7. (Walt) Whitman
8. Maccabee or Maccabaeus
9. Orthodox

And the Inspiration Word is:

1	2	3	4	5	6	7	8	9
W	H	O	L	E	S	O	M	E

QUIZ #15

WORDS AND MUSIC

1. According to the old spiritual, to spread the news that Jesus Christ is born, you should "Go tell it . . ." where?

2. What pop singer stirred up some controversy when she used religious imagery in the video of her song "Like a Prayer"?

3. The middle name of what Austrian composer means "loved by God"?

_____

_____

_____

Bonus: According to another old spiritual, what is it that "nobody knows but Jesus"?

Bonus: "I Don't Know How to Love Him" is Mary Magdalene's lament in what Broadway musical?

Bonus: By the time that composer wrote "God Is Our Refuge," he was considered a genius. Did he write it when he was nine, nineteen, or twenty-nine years old?

Quiz #15 — WORDS AND MUSIC

4. What folk-singing trio could have called themselves "Two Apostles and the Blessed Virgin"?

5. In what Gounod opera does the title character, an old man, sign a contract with Mephistopheles, who makes him young again?

6. What Christmas carol includes the line "O tidings of comfort and joy"?

Your Answers

_____ _____ _____
_____ _____ _____

Bonus: What singer-songwriter has the same last name as the original name of the apostle Peter?

Bonus: French composer Francis Poulenc wrote an opera about members of a religious order and called it *Dialogues of the . . .* what?

Bonus: What Christmas carol includes the line "Let earth receive her King"?

Words and Music

7. Following are three phrases, including one from the Bible. Each phrase has the same word missing. You fill in the missing word.

____ of Solomon

____ and dance

____ of Bernadette

8. The following headline might have appeared if there were tabloid newspapers in biblical times. You identify the event the headline describes.

JAKE NAPS AND DREAMS: IN HIS SLEEP HE SINGS "STAIRWAY TO PARADISE"

9. The following sentence contains the hidden last name of the composer of *The Saint of Bleecker Street*. You find the hidden name.

WHY IS MAME NOT TIDY?

Bonus:
Following are three more phrases, including one from the Bible, and each with the same word missing. You fill in the missing word.

____ of plenty

French ____

The ____ of my salvation

Bonus:
When "Jake" in the above headline is reunited with his brother, does the brother forgive him, shun him, or kill him?

Bonus:
The following sentence contains the hidden last name of the composer of *Stabat Mater*. You find the hidden name.

WAS EROS SINISTER?

Quiz #15 — Words and Music

10. Rearrange the letters in the word DRIVE to get the last name of the composer of *Nabucco*, an opera based on the biblical story of Nebuchadnezzar.

11. Fans of the Edwin Hawkins Singers are fans of what kind of music?

12. What 1960s rock opera about a messianic figure was written by The Who?

Bonus: Rearrange the letters in the word GLARE to get the last name of the composer of *Pomp and Circumstance*, who played the organ for church services at England's Worcester Cathedral.

Bonus: What country music quartet, named for a city in Tennessee, started out as a gospel group?

Bonus: The main author of that rock opera wrote it after becoming disenchanted with Eastern mysticism. Name him.

102

WORDS AND MUSIC — Quiz #15

13. What entertainer's *Piano Man* album featured the song "Traveling Prayer"?

14. The title of a World War II song, inspired by the words of a chaplain, suggested that soldiers should praise the Lord and pass the *what*?

15. What prayer, based on the salutation of an angel and the words of Elisabeth to the Virgin Mary, has been set to music by such composers as Schubert, Brahms, and Rossini?

Bonus:
John Denver had a big hit song called "Thank God I'm a . . ." what?

Bonus:
Which former member of the Beatles wrote the 1970s hit song called "My Sweet Lord"?

Bonus:
According to "The Battle Hymn of the Republic," "Christ was born across the sea" in the beauty of what flowers?

WORDS AND MUSIC

INSPIRATION WORD
(11 LETTERS)

___ ___ ___ ___ ___ ___ ___ ___ ___ ___ ___
1   2   3   4   5   6   7   8   9   10 11

The correct answer to each question begins with one of the letters in the Inspiration Word, and the number in parentheses after the question tells you in which space (above) to insert that letter. Guess each answer and insert its first letter in the proper space. If your answers are right, you'll soon to be able to identify the Inspiration Word.

On the *Inspiration, Please!* television show, this eleven-letter word was guessed after only six letters.

1. The English king who led the Third Crusade was known as Richard the... what? (7)
2. What famous prayer can be found in the Gospels of Matthew and Luke? (3)
3. Solomon built his temple with cedar trees from what country? (6)
4. The name of what country in Central America means "The Savior" in Spanish? (9)
5. What actress played the title role in the TV series called *The Flying Nun*? (1)
6. In the Book of Numbers, the Lord tells Moses to make two musical instruments of silver and hammered work. What kind of instruments were they? (11)
7. Who founded the Church of the Foursquare Gospel and was the foremost female evangelist of her day? (8)
8. Who does Genesis describe as "a mighty hunter" and "the first on earth to be a mighty man"? (10)
9. The cross of St. George appears on the flag of Great Britain. What is the popular name of that flag? (2)
10. Name the island nation whose state church is the Evangelical Lutheran Church and whose capital is Reykjavik. (5)
11. How many bishops are there in a chess game? (4)

Answers to Quiz #15

Words and Music

1. On the mountain
2. Madonna
3. Wolfgang Amadeus Mozart (*Amadeus* is Latin for "loved by God.")
4. Peter, Paul, and Mary
5. *Faust*
6. "God Rest Ye Merry, Gentlemen"
7. Song
8. Jacob dreams of a ladder between Heaven and earth.
9. Why is MaME NOT TIdy? ([Gian-Carlo] Menotti)
10. (Giuseppe) Verdi
11. Gospel
12. *Tommy*
13. Billy Joel
14. The ammunition. The song is "Praise the Lord and Pass the Ammunition.")
15. "Ave Maria"

Answers to Bonus Questions:

1. "The trouble I've seen"
2. *Jesus Christ Superstar*
3. Nine
4. Paul Simon
5. Carmelites
6. "Joy to the World"
7. Horn
8. Forgive him. When they are reunited, Esau forgives Jacob.
9. Was (E)ROS SINIster? ([Gioacchino] Rossini)
10. (Sir Edward) Elgar
11. The Oak Ridge Boys
12. Peter Townshend
13. Country Boy
14. George Harrison
15. Lilies

Inspiration Word Answers

1. Lion-Hearted
2. The Lord's Prayer
3. Lebanon
4. El Salvador
5. (Sally) Field
6. Trumpets
7. (Aimee Semple) McPherson
8. Nimrod
9. Union Jack or Union Flag
10. Iceland
11. Four

And the Inspiration Word is:

1	2	3	4	5	6	7	8	9	10	11
F	U	L	F	I	L	L	M	E	N	T

Quiz #16

This and That and Wise Men, Too

1. The Wise Men brought three gifts to the baby Jesus, including what precious metal?

2. Catholics use a string of beads for counting prayers during their recitation. What are the beads called?

3. The English city of Salisbury is famous for its cathedral and for being close to what prehistoric monument on Salisbury Plain?

Bonus:
The Wise Men also brought frankincense to the newborn Jesus. Is frankincense animal, vegetable, or mineral?

Bonus:
"Phylacteries" are small cubes containing biblical verses that a man straps to his forehead and arm during his morning prayers. To what religion does the man belong?

Bonus:
Christ Church, Trinity, and All Souls are colleges of what university in England?

This and That and Wise Men, Too

Quiz #19

4. What newspaper advice column sounds as if it could be called "Dear Monastery"?

5. Who was the pope during World War II?

6. What author had to go into hiding after writing *The Satanic Verses*?

Bonus: The first name of Ms. Hill, the country music star, means "belief and confidence in God." What is her first name?

Bonus: Which pope continued the papal policy of strict neutrality and impartiality during World War I

Bonus: What author of *A Child's Garden of Verses* wrote "Requiem," the poem that is inscribed on his gravestone?

Quiz #16 — This and That and Wise Men, Too

7. Following are three phrases, including one from the Bible. Each phrase has the same word missing. You fill in the missing word.

____ those who curse you

____ this house

God ____ America

8. The following headline might have appeared if there were tabloid newspapers in the year A.D. 800. You identify the event the headline describes.

LEO PICKS CHARLEY AS NEW C.E.O.

9. The following sentence contains the hidden name of a mythological goddess. You find the name.

IT AFFECTS EVEN US.

Your Answers

Bonus:
Following are three phrases, including one from the Bible, and each with the same word missing. You fill in the missing word.

____ variety

Covent ____

The ____ of God

Bonus:
The "Charley" in the above headline defeated the Saxons, preparing the way for the religious conversion of what country?

Bonus:
The following sentence contains the hidden name of another mythological goddess. You find the name.

EVERY MINER VALUES IT.

This and That and Wise Men, Too

10. Rearrange the letters in the word CANED to get what, according to Judges, the daughters of Shiloh came out to do.

11. What well-known spiritual includes the line, "Comin' for to carry me home"?

12. Joan of Arc was born in what country?

Bonus: Rearrange the letters in the word IRAN to get what, according to James, Elijah prayed it wouldn't do.

Bonus: What spiritual includes the line, "I want to cross over into camp ground"?

Bonus: Joan of Arc was revered in her native land for fighting against the domination of what country?

Quiz #16 — THIS AND THAT AND WISE MEN, TOO

13. What language, spoken by Jews around the world, is a mixture of Slavic, Hebrew, and several high German dialects?

14. Three of the four Gospels are known as the Synoptic Gospels. Which one is not?

15. What brand of dishwashing liquid shares its name with the bird that is a symbol of peace?

Your Answers

_____

_____

_____

Bonus: In the Sanskrit language, does the name Buddha mean enlightened, peaceful, or powerful?

Bonus: Which of the four Gospel writers was known as a "publican"?

Bonus: The name of what brand of dishwashing liquid is what, according to Acts, the disciples were filled with.

THIS AND THAT AND WISE MEN, TOO

QUIZ #16

INSPIRATION WORD
(10 LETTERS)

YOUR ANSWERS

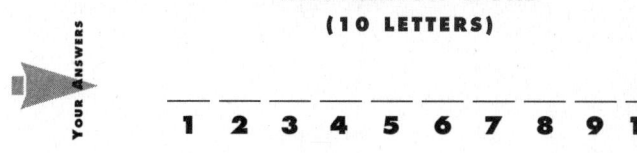

___ ___ ___ ___ ___ ___ ___ ___ ___ ___
 1   2   3   4   5   6   7   8   9   10

The correct answer to each question begins with one of the letters in the Inspiration Word, and the number in parentheses after the question tells you in which space (above) to insert that letter. Guess each answer, and insert its first letter in the proper space. If your answers are right, you'll soon be able to identify the Inspiration Word.

On the *Inspiration, Please!* television show, this Inspiration Word was guessed after nine letters.

1. What American inventor said, "Genius is one percent inspiration and ninety-nine percent perspiration"? (4)
2. Who is the current cardinal of the Archdiocese of New York? (6)
3. Getting drunk on a beer called "chicha" was a religious ritual among what Indian people who built an empire in Peru? (8)
4. Rex Harrison played Pope Julius II in a film called *The Agony and the . . .* what? (2)
5. In what month is All Saints' Day? (3)
6. Passover bread is called unleavened because it does not contain what? (10)
7. Fill in the blank in this line from a well-known hymn: "Will there be any _____ in my crown?" (7)
8. Proverbs tells us that a beautiful woman without discretion is like a gold *what* in a swine's snout? (5)
9. In the Gospel of Matthew, Jesus says, "My house shall be called a house of prayer, but ye have made it a den of . . ." what? (9)
10. According to the book of Judges, what judge was also a wheat farmer? (1)

ANSWERS TO QUIZ #16

THIS AND THAT AND WISE MEN, TOO

1. Gold
2. The Rosary
3. Stonehenge
4. "Dear Abby" (An abbey is a monastery.)
5. Pope Pius XII
6. Salman Rushdie
7. Bless
8. Charlemagne is crowned Emperor by Pope Leo III.
9. It affects eVEN US. (Venus)
10. Dance
11. "Swing Low, Sweet Chariot"
12. France
13. Yiddish
14. The Gospel of John
15. Dove

ANSWERS TO BONUS QUESTIONS:

1. Vegetable (It's a tree resin used for incense.)
2. Judaism
3. Oxford
4. Faith Hill
5. Benedict XV
6. Robert Louis Stevenson
7. Garden
8. Germany
9. Every MINER VAlues it. (Minerva)
10. Rain
11. "Deep River"
12. England
13. Enlightened
14. Matthew (A publican was a tax-collector.)
15. Joy

INSPIRATION WORD ANSWERS

1. (Thomas Alva) Edison
2. (John Cardinal) O'Connor
3. Incas
4. Ecstasy
5. November (It's November 1.)
6. Yeast
7. Stars
8. Ring
9. Thieves
10. Gideon

And the Inspiration Word is:

1	2	3	4	5	6	7	8	9	10
G	E	N	E	R	O	S	I	T	Y

Quiz #17

MURDERERS, ANGELS, ETC.

1. Who was the first person in the Bible to commit a murder?

2. Spelled with six letters, it's a mounted gun. Spelled with five letters, it's the body of ecclesiastical law. What is it?

3. What Sunday does a religious Christian know like the inner surface of his hand?

Bonus: Who ordered that all infant boys in Bethlehem should be killed?

Bonus: Spelled one way, it's a weapon that's thrown, shot, or propelled. Spelled another way, it's a book of prayers or devotions. What is it?

Bonus: What do we call the laws designed to enforce certain forms of morality on Sunday?

Quiz #17 — MURDERERS, ANGELS, ETC.

4. The English word "angel" comes from the Greek word *angelos*. What does *angelos* mean?

5. When Noah was in his ark, how long did it rain?

6. Ascension Day always falls on what day of the week?

Your Answers

_____
_____

Bonus:
Thrones, powers, and seraphim are all orders of angels. Of the three, which is the highest order?

Bonus:
How long was Moses on Mount Sinai receiving the Ten Commandments?

Bonus:
According to Scandinavian mythology, who is the God of Thunder for whom Thursday is named?

Murderers, Angels, Etc. — Quiz #17

7. Following are three phrases, including one from the Bible. Each phrase has the same word missing. You fill in the missing word.

_____ cobra

Their _____ will pass on before them

_____ of beasts

8. The following headline might have appeared if there were tabloid newspapers in 1534. You identify the event the headline describes.

POPE SAYS "NO SPLIT" SO HANK STARTS BRAND-NEW GAME

9. The following sentence contains the hidden name of a biblical character. You find the name.

IS BASIL A SPICE?

Bonus:
Following are three more phrases, including one from the Bible, and each with the same word missing. You fill in the blank.

A man after his own _____

_____ and soul

_____ attack

Bonus:
In 1534, "Hank" in the headline above insisted that his government pass an act making his church a separate institution headed by himself. What was the act called?

Bonus:
The following sentence contains the hidden name of another biblical character. You find the name.

WATCH DESI MONKEY AROUND.

Quiz #17 — MURDERERS, ANGELS, ETC.

10. Rearrange the letters in word MOLE to get the name of the patron saint of sailors.

11. What world-famous chapel is named for Pope Sixtus IV?

12. If you placed a help wanted ad for a fisherman, would Andrew, Lazarus, or Shebna be most likely to apply?

Your Answers

Bonus:
Rearrange the letters in the word TACO to get what Goliath wore that was the weight of 5,000 shekels of bronze.

Bonus:
The world's largest church was recently built in which African country: Liberia, Ghana, or the Ivory Coast?

Bonus:
If you placed a help wanted ad for a tentmaker, would Amos, Cornelius, or Paul be most likely to apply?

Murderers, Angels, Etc.

13. The Caribbean island named St. Thomas belongs to what country?

14. What is the only book of the New Testament that starts with the letter "L"?

15. What part of the name Abraham is not kosher?

Bonus:
The name of which of the United States Virgin Islands includes the French word for "cross"?

Bonus:
What is the only book of the New Testament that stars with the letter "H"?

Bonus:
The name of what northeastern state begins with a Roman Catholic church service?

Quiz #17

MURDERERS, ANGELS, ETC.

INSPIRATION WORD
(8 LETTERS)

YOUR ANSWERS

___ ___ ___ ___ ___ ___ ___ ___
 1   2   3   4   5   6   7   8

The correct answer to each question begins with one of the letters in the Inspiration Word, and the number in parentheses after the question tells you in which space (above) to insert that letter. Guess each answer, and insert its first letter in the proper space. If your answers are right, you'll soon be able to identify the Inspiration Word.

On the *Inspiration, Please!* television show, this Inspiration Word was guessed after seven letters.

1. Add one letter to the word "immorality," and you'll get what word meaning "eternal life"? (6)
2. Jacob's third son had the same name as Mr. Strauss, the blue jeans maker. What's the name? (2)
3. Which of Columbus's ships was named for a saint? (5)
4. "An atheist is a guy who watches a Notre Dame–Southern Methodist University football game and doesn't care who wins." Those are the words of what man who twice defeated Adlai Stevenson for president? (3)
5. St. Augustine's College is in Raleigh, the capital of what state? (7)
6. Bors and Percival were two of the three knights of the Round Table who found the Holy Grail. But the third is even better known. Name him. (8)
7. Saint Patrick is said to have rid Ireland of what reptiles? (4)
8. The chorus of what hymn begins with the words "Glory, glory, hallelujah"? (1)

118

Answers to Quiz #17

Murderers, Angels, Etc.

1. Cain (He killed his brother, Abel.)
2. Cannon/Canon
3. Palm Sunday
4. Messenger
5. Forty days and forty nights
6. Thursday
7. King
8. Henry VIII establishes the Church of England after Pope Leo won't annul his marriage to Catherine of Aragon.
9. Is baSIL A Spice? (Silas)
10. Elmo
11. The Sistine Chapel at the Vatican
12. Andrew
13. The United States
14. Luke
15. Ham (AbraHAM)

Answers to Bonus Questions:

1. Herod
2. Missile/Missal
3. Blue laws
4. Seraphim
5. Forty days and forty nights
6. Thor
7. Heart
8. The Act of Supremacy
9. Watch DeSI MONkey around. (Simon)
10. Coat
11. The Ivory Coast
12. Paul
13. St. Croix
14. Hebrews
15. Massachusetts (MASSachusetts)

Inspiration Word Answers

1. Immortality
2. Levi
3. Santa María
4. (Dwight David) Eisenhower
5. North Carolina
6. Galahad
7. Snakes
8. ("The) Battle Hymn of the Republic"

And the Inspiration Word is:

B L E S S I N G
1 2 3 4 5 6 7 8

Quiz #18

Let's Get Theory-ous

1. Who studied to become an Anglican priest before he became a naturalist and pioneered the theory of evolution?

2. Which islands in the Pacific sound as if they were discovered by the wisest king in the Old Testament?

3. In 1966, what famous English cathedral become even more famous as the title of a hit song?

Bonus:
What Russian dictator studied to be a Jesuit priest but was expelled for reading the books of Karl Marx and Victor Hugo?

Bonus:
In the days before income taxes, that same wise king received gifts worth about three and a half million dollars from what queen?

Bonus:
In 1968, what rock group had a number one hit called "Lady Madonna"?

LET'S GET THEORY-OUS

Quiz #18

4. On what day of the week did Jesus' resurrection take place?

5. If a clergyman has a "cassock," does he read it, wear it, or lie down on it?

6. The people who belong to what church are commonly called "Moonies"?

Bonus:
In the New Testament, Jesus says, "Follow me, and I will make you fishers of . . ." what?

Bonus:
If a nun wears a "wimple," does she wear it on her head, on her arm, or around her waist?

Bonus:
The evangelist who heads the church of the Moonies comes from what country?

Quiz #18 — LET'S GET THEORY-OUS

7. Following are three phrases, including one from the Bible. Each phrase has the same word missing. You fill in the missing word.

_____ glory

The _____ star rises

The _____ after

8. The following headline might have appeared if there were tabloid newspapers in the early sixteenth century. You identify the event the headline describes.

MIKE LIES DOWN ON THE JOB SO HE CAN PAINT 70 FEET UP!

9. The following sentence contains the hidden name of a character in the Old Testament. You find the hidden name.

I HAD A VIDEOTAPE.

Your Answers

_____   _____   _____

Bonus:
Following are three more phrases, including one from the Bible, and each with the same word missing. You fill in the missing word.

Speaking into the _____

Clear the _____

Up in the _____

Bonus:
In 1972, a man damaged which one of "Mike's" works by attacking it with a hammer?

Bonus:
The following sentence contains another hidden name from the Old Testament. You find the name.

LET'S WATCH LISA ACT.

122

Let's Get Theory-ous

10. Rearrange the letters in the word BALM to get the animal that Exodus says is without blemish.

11. What Roman emperor, the nephew of Caligula, was known for his mistreatment of Christians?

12. What comedian named Danny was closely associated with the St. Jude Children's Research Hospital?

Bonus:
Rearrange the letters in the word REPEL to get one of the diseased people healed by Jesus.

Bonus:
In what popular 1951 film with a Latin title did Peter Ustinov play the role of Nero?

Bonus:
What comedian named Danny helped children around the world as a spokesman for UNICEF, the United Nations International Children's Emergency Fund?

Quiz #18 — LET'S GET THEORY-OUS

13. Who is the most famous former headmistress of St. Mary's School in Calcutta, India?

14. It is considered sacred, and more than fifty thousand pilgrims climb to its summit each year. Name this highest mountain in Japan.

15. Which one of the Ten Commandments was broken by Hester Prynne in *The Scarlet Letter*?

Your Answers

Bonus: The play and film called *Children of a Lesser God* take place in what kind of school?

Bonus: Its stone ornaments, figures, and gargoyles are so high up that it's said only an angel can admire their details. Name this church in the heart of Paris.

Bonus: One of the Ten Commandments says, "Thou shalt not bear false witness against . . ." whom?

124

LET'S GET THEORY-OUS

INSPIRATION WORD
(8 LETTERS)

___ ___ ___ ___ ___ ___ ___ ___
 1   2   3   4   5   6   7   8

The correct answer to each question begins with one of the letters in the Inspiration Word, and the number in parentheses after the question tells you in which space (above) to insert that letter. Guess each answer, and insert its first letter in the proper space. If your answers are right, you'll soon be able to identify the Inspiration word.

On the *Inspiration, Please!* television show, this Inspiration Word was guessed after seven letters.

1. According to Leviticus, what did the people of Israel burn in order to make a sweet-smelling smoke in the temple? (6)
2. "Thou Art Ruler of the Minds of All People" is the national anthem in what country, where more than 80 percent of the people are Hindu? (4)
3. In Salt Lake City, what do Mormons call the domed structure that houses their huge organ and choir? (3)
4. In the song "The Twelve Days of Christmas," there are how many drummers drumming? (7)
5. The book of Isaiah says, "All we like sheep have gone astray." The drinking song that says, "We are poor little sheep who have gone astray," is associated with what university? (8)
6. An abbot is the head of a monastery. What is the equivalent title of the female head of a convent of nuns? (2)
7. Ms. Cole, the pop singer, has a first name that means "Born at Christmastide." What is her first name? (1)
8. Who worked as a mission preacher, but is much better known as a legendary painter who cut off his own ear? (5)

Answers to Quiz #18

Let's Get Theory-ous

1. Charles Darwin
2. The Solomon Islands
3. Winchester Cathedral
4. Sunday (That's why Sunday is the Christian Sabbath.)
5. He wears it. It's a long, close-fitting garment.)
6. Unification Church
7. Morning
8. Michelangelo paints the ceiling of the Sistine Chapel while lying on his back.
9. I haD A VIDeo tape. (David)
10. Lamb
11. Nero
12. Danny Thomas
13. Mother Teresa
14. Mount Fuji or Fujiyama
15. Thou shalt not commit adultery.

Answers to Bonus Questions:

1. Joseph Stalin
2. The Queen of Sheba
3. The Beatles
4. Men
5. On her head. It's a headcloth.
6. Korea or South Korea
7. Air
8. *The Pietà*
9. Let's watch (L)ISA ACt. (Isaac)
10. Leper
11. *Quo Vadis*
12. Danny Kaye
13. A school for the deaf
14. Cathedral of Notre Dame
15. Thy neighbor

Inspiration Word Answers

1. Incense
2. India
3. Tabernacle
4. Twelve
5. Yale
6. Abbess
7. Natalie
8. (Vincent) van Gogh

And the Inspiration Word is:

```
  1   2   3   4   5   6   7   8
  N   A   T   I   V   I   T   Y
```

Quiz #19

Is There a Doctrine in the House?

1. What do you call the doctrine or belief that there is only one God?

2. What biblical character got up early in the morning and made burnt offerings as sacrifices, in case any of his sons had sinned?

3. For more than 130 years, God's name has been used on most American coins in what four-word motto?

Bonus: What do you call a form of government in which God is recognized as the supreme civil ruler?

Bonus: That biblical character came from a land spelled with only two letters. Was it Uz, Oz, or Iz?

Bonus: According to the song made popular by Bing Crosby, what coins does it rain, "every time it rains"?

Quiz #19: Is There a Doctrine in the House?

4. Augustus Montague Toplady and Thomas Hantings wrote the well-known hymn whose title begins with the word "Rock." What's the full title?

5. What religious group is named for Jacob Ammann, who led them in breaking away from the Swiss Mennonites in the seventeenth century?

6. At the Last Supper, when Jesus told his disciples "This is my body" and "This is my blood," to what was he referring?

Your Answers

Bonus: The title of another well-known hymn, this one with a melody from a Croatian folk song, begins with the word "Glorious." What's the full title?

Bonus: What do members of that religious group call the practice of completely avoiding excommunicated members?

Bonus: At the Last Supper, Jesus told his disciples that one of them would do what?

Is There a Doctrine in the House?

7. Following are three phrases, including one from the Bible. Each phrase has the same word missing. You fill in the missing word.

Perfect love casts out _____

Cape _____

_____ of Flying

8. The following headline might have appeared if there were tabloid newspapers in the year 950 B.C. You identify the event the headline describes.

IT'S A FIRST FOR SOL!
HIS CONSTRUCTION CO.
MAKES HISTORY!

9. The following sentence contains the hidden name of several popes. You find the name.

THREE ELEPHANTS
HAVE SIX TUSKS.

Bonus:
Following are three more phrases, including one from the Bible, and each with the same word missing. You fill in the missing word.

_____ food

Body and _____

He poured out his _____

Bonus:
Who were "Sol's" parents?

Bonus:
The following sentence contains another hidden name of several popes. You find the name.

IT'S FROM ART IN CHICAGO.

Quiz #19 — Is There a Doctrine in the House?

10. Rearrange the letters in the word LINE to get the name of a river that the Bible says was turned into blood.

11. What city in Hungary sounds like an Indian religious leader's nuisance?

12. In what country did King Henry IV issue the Edict of Nantes, which guaranteed religious and civil liberties to the Huguenots?

Your Answers

Bonus: Rearrange the letters in the word ERECT to get the name of the Greek Island where the churches were supervised by Titus.

Bonus: What synonym for Heaven sounds like what a crapshooter throws?

Bonus: In 1624, what cardinal became prime minister of that country and took charge of the kingdom?

130

Is There a Doctrine in the House?

Quiz #19

13. Let's play "Occupation, Please." Was Mary's husband a weaver, a priest, or a carpenter?

14. What character on the TV sitcom *Taxi* had the same name as a potato pancake that Jewish people eat on Chanukah?

15. Clement Moore wrote one of the most famous of all Christmas poems. What are its first five words?

Bonus:
Was Deborah a midwife, a judge, or a seamstress?

Bonus:
A "shammash" is a custodian of a synagogue. But on Chanukah, it has another meaning. Is it a bell, a book, or a candle?

Bonus:
Who wrote *How the Grinch Stole Christmas*?

131

Quiz #19

IS THERE A DOCTRINE IN THE HOUSE?

INSPICATION WORD
(10 LETTERS)

YOUR ANSWERS

___ ___ ___ ___ ___ ___ ___ ___ ___ ___
 1   2   3   4   5   6   7   8   9   10

The correct answer to each question begins with one of the letters in the Inspiration Word, and the number in parentheses after the question tells you in which space (above) to insert that letter. Guess each answer, and insert its first letter in the proper space. If your answers are right, you'll soon be able to identify the Inspiration Word.

On the *Inspiration, Please!* television show, this Inspiration Word was guessed after eight letters.

1. According to folklore, when the god who supports the earth changes his position, what kind of natural disaster occurs? (4)
2. In a Jack Nicholson movie, Susan Sarandon, Michelle Pfeiffer, and Cher played witches of what town? (10)
3. Who is famous for writing many fables with morals, including "The Tortoise and the Hare"? (7)
4. The saint who is said to have preached to the birds when people would not listen was Saint Francis of what Italian city? (2)
5. Fill in the blank in the title of this Ernest Hemingway novel that takes its name from the Book of Ecclesiastes: *The Sun Also* _____. (5)
6. In the nineteenth century, on the Hawaiian island of Molokai, Father Damien was a Belgian Catholic missionary to what kind of colony? (9)
7. The body of Mother Cabrini, the first United States citizen to be made a saint by the Catholic Church, is in St. Frances Xavier Cabrini High School in what city? (6)
8. A priest, a bishop, and a pope—Johnny Priest, Charlie Bishop, and Dave Pope—are all names associated with what professional sport? (3)
9. Religious officials usually perform what ceremony at which a king or queen is crowned? (8)
10. According to the song, "All I want for Christmas . . ." is how many front teeth? (1)

ANSWERS TO QUIZ #19

IS THERE A DOCTRINE IN THE HOUSE?

1. Monotheism
2. Job
3. In God We Trust
4. "Rock of Ages"
5. The Amish
6. Bread and wine
7. Fear
8. Solomon builds the first temple.
9. Three elephants have SIX TUSks. (Sixtus)
10. Nile
11. Budapest (Buddha pest!)
12. France
13. Carpenter
14. Latka
15. "Twas the Night Before Christmas"

ANSWERS TO BONUS QUESTIONS:

1. Theocracy
2. Uz
3. Pennies (The song is "Pennies from Heaven.")
4. "Glorious Things of Thee Are Spoken"
5. Shunning
6. Betray him
7. Soul
8. David and Bathsheba
9. It's froM ART IN Chicago. (Martin)
10. Crete
11. Paradise (Pair o' dice!)
12. Cardinal Richelieu
13. Judge
14. A candle. It's the candle used to light the other Chanukah candles.
15. Dr. Seuss (Theodor Geisel)

INSPIRATION WORD ANSWERS

1. Earthquake
2. Eastwick (The film is *The Witches of Eastwick*.)
3. Aesop
4. Assisi
5. Rises
6. Leper
7. New York City
8. Baseball
9. Coronation
10. Two

And the Inspiration Word is:

1	2	3	4	5	6	7	8	9	10
T	A	B	E	R	N	A	C	L	E

Quiz #20

Age-Old Questions

1. What artist became the architect of St. Peter's in Rome when he was over seventy years old?

2. In Einstein's famous equation, it's the "M." In a Catholic church it's a celebration of the Eucharist. What is it?

3. What is the oldest civil rights organization in the United States?

Your Answers

Bonus: London's St. Paul's Cathedral was designed by what famous British architect?

Bonus: Theologically speaking, it's a region on the border of Heaven and Hell. Musically speaking, it's a dance of the West Indies. What is it?

Bonus: Was that civil rights organization founded in 1859, 1909, or 1959?

134

Age-Old Questions

Quiz #20

4. What is the name of eight popes *and* the kind of cowboy John Travolta played in a movie?

5. In Jerusalem, at what wall do Jews gather for prayers and lamentation?

6. Our Lady of Guadelupe is the patron saint of what North American country?

Bonus: What is the name of thirteen popes, all of whom sound "not guilty"?

Bonus: What is the name of the word or formula that is recited or sung by a meditating Hindu?

Bonus: Saint Andrew is the patron saint of what division of the United Kingdom?

Quiz #20 — Age-Old Questions

7. Following are three phrases, including one from the Bible. Each phrase has the same word missing. You fill in the missing word.

____ roll

In holiness and ____

Badge of ____

8. The following headline might have appeared if there were tabloid newspapers in biblical times. You identify the event the headline describes.

WIFE PEEKED, SO NOW SHE'S A PILLAR OF SOCIETY

9. The following sentence contains the hidden name of a biblical place. You find the place.

IS INA IN TOWN TODAY?

Bonus:
Following are three more phrases, including one from the Bible, and each with the same word missing. You fill in the missing word.

A man of his ____

____ processor

The ____ is very near you.

Bonus:
When the wife in the headline peeked, she and her husband were fleeing from what city?

Bonus:
The following sentence contains the hidden name of another biblical place. You find the place.

THE BABE LOVED HIS FANS.

136

Age-Old Questions

Quiz #20

10. Rearrange the letters in the word DANGER to get what Eden was.

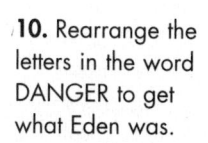

11. The name of what Texas city is Spanish for "Saint Anthony"?

12. President Jimmy Carter confessed to having had which of the seven deadly sins in his heart?

Bonus: Rearrange the letters in the word HATED to get what, according to Revelation, was the name of him who sat on a pale horse.

Bonus: The name of what Texas city is Latin for "body of Christ"?

Bonus: Which of the seven deadly sins is defined as "excessive eating and drinking"?

Quiz #20 — Age-Old Questions

13. To what weapon was Jesus referring when he said that he who lives by it, dies by it?

14. Until he or she has taken vows, a person who has been received into a religious order for a period of probation is called what?

15. What classic novel begins with the line "Call me Ishmael"?

Your Answers

Bonus: Four soldiers cast lots for something that belonged to Jesus. What did they want?

Bonus: Some religious orders are "cloistered." Does the word "cloistered" mean silent, strict, or secluded?

Bonus: Name one of the parents of the biblical Ishmael.

138

AGE-OLD QUESTIONS

QUIZ #20

INSPIRATION WORD
(9 LETTERS)

YOUR ANSWERS

___ ___ ___ ___ ___ ___ ___ ___ ___
1   2   3   4   5   6   7   8   9

The correct answer to each question begins with one of the letters in the Inspiration Word, and the number in parentheses after the question tells you in which space (above) to insert that letter. Guess each answer and insert its first letter in the proper space. If your answers are right, you'll soon be able to identify the Inspiration Word.

On the *Inspiration, Please!* television show, this Inspiration Word was guessed after five letters.

1. According to the Beatitudes in Matthew's Gospel, who is blessed "for they shall inherit the earth"? (4)
2. When the pope speaks on matters of faith or morals, he is divinely protected from error by the doctrine called "papal . . ." what? (7)
3. He wrote *Dynamo* and *Days Without End,* two plays in which characters seeking meaning to their lives turn to religion. He also wrote *Long Day's Journey into Night.* Name him. (2)
4. What leader of the Mormon Church had children by sixteen wives? (9)
5. What planet is named for the Roman messenger of the gods? (3)
6. What Hebrew leader of the fifth century B.C., for whom a book of the Old Testament is named, wept when he heard that the walls of Jerusalem were still in ruins? (6)
7. The artifact reported to be Jesus' burial cloth is known as the Shroud of what Italian city? (8)
8. The name of what mythological animal, with a horn in its forehead, was mentioned in early Bibles but is now translated as "wild ox"? (5)
9. She was called "The Angel of the Battlefield," and her last name was Barton. What was her first name? (1)

ANSWERS TO QUIZ #20

AGE-OLD QUESTIONS

1. Michelangelo
2. Mass
3. The NAACP (National Association for the Advancement of Colored People)
4. Urban (The Travolta film was *Urban Cowboy*.)
5. The Wailing Wall or the Western Wall
6. Mexico
7. Honor
8. Lot's wife, told not to turn around, does so and turns into a pillar of salt.
9. (I)S INA In town today? (Sinai)
10. Garden
11. San Antonio
12. Lust
13. The sword
14. A novice or novitiate
15. *Moby Dick*

ANSWERS TO BONUS QUESTIONS:

1. Christopher Wren
2. Limbo
3. 1909
4. Innocent
5. Mantra
6. Scotland
7. Word
8. Sodom
9. The BABE Loved his fans. (Babel)
10. Death
11. Corpus Christi
12. Gluttony
13. His clothing (or his robe or tunic)
14. Secluded
15. Hagar or Abram (or Abraham)

INSPIRATION WORD ANSWERS

1. Meek
2. Infallibility
3. (Eugene) O'Neill
4. (Brigham) Young
5. Mercury
6. Nehemiah
7. Turin
8. Unicorn
9. Clara

And the Inspiration Word is:

1	2	3	4	5	6	7	8	9
C	O	M	M	U	N	I	T	Y

Quiz #21

Major Leagues and Minor Prophets

1. If you took the names of the major league baseball teams literally, the most heavenly team would be the California Angels. What National League team would be most likely to elect the next pope?

2. The last twelve books of the Old Testament are named for the twelve minor prophets. Which book is the *last* of the twelve?

3. According to superstition, you'll keep the Devil at a distance if you throw a little bit of what over your left shoulder?

Bonus: What National League team would be most likely to recruit Goliath?

Bonus: The word *prophet* comes from the Greek. Does it mean one who prays, one who proclaims, or one who plants?

Bonus: According to superstition, where will you get a blister if you tell a lie?

141

Quiz #21 — MAJOR LEAGUES AND MINOR PROPHETS

4. Though he is anything but sinister, what word for a clergyman rhymes with "sinister"?

5. Jesus said it is necessary to become like a little child in order to enter . . . what?

6. G.K. Chesterton wrote a series of popular mysteries about a wise and whimsical detective named Father . . . who?

Your Answers

Bonus:
He can be a beacon of light for many. What elected or appointed church official rhymes with "beacon"?

Bonus:
Jesus said you need faith the size of a mustard seed in order to move . . . what?

Bonus:
Harry Kemelman wrote mysteries about a clergyman-detective named David Small. What was David Small's religion?

MAJOR LEAGUES AND MINOR PROPHETS

7. Following are three phrases, including one from the Bible. Each phrase has the same word missing. You fill in the missing word.

The Great _____

He shall _____ the spoil

_____ and conquer

8. The following headline might have appeared if there were tabloid newspapers in biblical times. You identify the event the headline describes.

"NEBBISH" IS BURNED UP BECAUSE THREE MEN HE FIRED ARE NOT!

9. The following sentence contains the hidden name of a minor prophet. You find the name.

HE CHOSE A BEAUTIFUL WIFE.

_____

_____

Bonus:
Following are three more phrases, including one from the Bible, and each has the same word missing. You fill in the missing word.

_____ fund

Position of _____

Those who _____ in riches

Bonus:
The "Nebbish" in the above headline probably built which of the Seven Wonders of the World?

Bonus:
The following sentence contains the hidden name of another minor prophet. You find the name.

TRY TO ACT IN A HUMBLE WAY.

143

Quiz #21 — MAJOR LEAGUES AND MINOR PROPHETS

10. Rearrange the letters in the word THORN to get the direction from which Job says fair weather comes.

11. If Newt Gingrich, Pat Buchanan, and Rush Limbaugh converted to Judaism, which of the three branches would they be most likely to join?

12. What was being returned to Jerusalem when David danced before the Lord?

Your Answers:

_____ _____ _____

Bonus: Rearrange the letters in the word LIVERS to get what, according to the book of Joel, the righteous were sold for.

Bonus: Was that branch of Judaism founded in Poland, Israel, or the United States?

Bonus: When David danced, he had an "ephod." Did he wear it, drink it, or pet it?

144

Major Leagues and Minor Prophets

Quiz #21

13. Ninety-five percent of the people of Cambodia belong to what religion?

_____

Bonus:
What is the name of the largest and best-preserved temple in the ruins of the Khmer empire in Cambodia?

14. In 1908, churches in Grafton, West Virginia, and in Philadelphia were the first to celebrate what holiday on the second Sunday in May?

_____

Bonus:
In 1910, a woman in Spokane, Washington, started what June holiday?

15. The book of Revelation tells of a period of 1,000 years during which Christ will reign on Earth. What is that 1,000-year period called?

_____

Bonus:
In Revelation, God uses what two Greek letters to describe himself?

Quiz #21

MAJOR LEAGUES AND MINOR PROPHETS

INSPIRATION WORD
(10 LETTERS)

YOUR ANSWERS

___ ___ ___ ___ ___ ___ ___ ___ ___ ___
 1   2   3   4   5   6   7   8   9   10

The correct answer to each question begins with one of the letters in the Inspiration Word, and the number in parentheses after the question tells you in which space (above) to insert that letter. Guess each answer and insert its first letter in the proper space. If your answers are right, you'll soon be able to identify the Inspiration Word.

On the *Inspiration, Please!* television show, this Inspiration Word was guessed after five letters.

1. In Genesis, the blind Isaac says, "The voice is Jacob's voice, but the hands are the hands of . . ." whom? (4)
2. What Christmas carol includes the line, "How still we see thee lie"? (9)
3. The last name of what former British prime minister is the same as the biblical place where the "tree of knowledge of good and evil" grew? (2)
4. What Victorian poet wrote a poem called "Holy Grail" as part of his collection titled *The Idylls of the King*? (7)
5. Fill in the blank in the title of this work by Dante that took readers on a journey through the afterlife: *The____Comedy*. (3)
6. Great Britain's greatest admiral and naval hero was the son of the rector of the local church. He was Lord . . . who? (10)
7. In what play and movie does Sir Thomas More's opposition to the divorce of King Henry VIII eventually lead to his execution? (5)
8. What saint, when he was sent to Rome in chains and thrown to the lions, said, "May I become agreeable bread to the Lord"? (8)
9. "Any God I ever felt in church, I brought in with me." Those are the words of Alice Walker, who wrote a popular novel called *The Color* . . . what? (6)
10. The paintings of what Dutch artist, whose last name was Van Ryn, include *The Good Samaritan* and *Jesus*? (1)

146

ANSWERS TO QUIZ #21

MAJOR LEAGUES AND MINOR PROPHETS

1. The Cardinals (St. Louis Cardinals)
2. Malachi
3. Salt
4. Minister
5. The Kingdom of Heaven
6. Father Brown
7. Divide
8. Shadrach, Meshach, and Abednego emerged unharmed from the fiery furnace of Nebuchadnezzar.
9. He cHOSE A beautiful wife. (Hosea)
10. North
11. Conservative (All three are members of the Republican party's conservative wing.)
12. The Ark of the Covenant or The Ark of the Lord
13. Buddhism
14. Mother's Day
15. Millennium

ANSWERS TO BONUS QUESTIONS:

1. The Giants (San Francisco Giants)
2. One who proclaims
3. On your tongue
4. Deacon
5. Mountains
6. Jewish (He is a rabbi.)
7. Trust
8. The Hanging Gardens of Babylon
9. Try to act iN A HUMble way. (Nahum)
10. Silver
11. The United States
12. He wore it. It's a richly embroidered vestment.
13. Angkor Wat
14. Father's Day
15. Alpha and omega

INSPIRATION WORD ANSWERS

1. Esau
2. "O Little Town of Bethlehem"
3. (Sir Anthony) Eden
4. (Alfred Lord) Tennyson
5. Divine
6. (Lord) Nelson
7. *(A) Man for All Seasons*
8. Ignatius
9. Purple
10. Rembrandt

And the Inspiration Word is:

1	2	3	4	5	6	7	8	9	10
R	E	D	E	M	P	T	I	O	N

Quiz #22

Plagues and Other Fun Stuff

1. Three of the ten plagues visited by God on the Egyptians involved insects. Name two of them.

2. It's only thyroid cartilage showing through the skin of a man's neck, but it sounds like something right out of the Garden of Eden. What is it?

3. A church offering called a "tithe" is equivalent to what percent?

Bonus: One of the ten plagues involved turning water into what?

Bonus: In mythology, Paris gave Aphrodite what apple inscribed "to the fairest"?

Bonus: If "polyandry" is legal in a country, it means women can do what?

Plagues and Other Fun Stuff

Quiz #22

4. Calvary, the hill outside Jerusalem on which Jesus was crucified, has another name. What is it?

5. The Pentateuch comprises how many books of the Old Testament?

6. Name the Quaker woman who was a social reformer and advocate for women's rights, but whose dollar didn't do so well.

Bonus: "Calvary" comes from the Latin word for what may have been the shape of the hill. Is it the Latin word for cloud, eagle, or skull?

Bonus: Based on their names alone, which of the books of the Pentateuch would appeal most to an accountant?

Bonus: On a United States dollar, does the word "God" appear on the side with Washington's picture, or on the other side? (No fair peeking!)

Quiz #22 — Plagues and Other Fun Stuff

7. Following are three phrases, including one from the Bible. Each phrase has the same word missing. You fill in the missing word.

Woe to you that _____ now

The last _____

Only when I _____

Your Answers:
_____
_____

Bonus:
Following are three more phrases, including one from the Bible, and each with the same word missing. You fill in the missing word.

_____ away camp

A spirit of deep _____

_____ tight

8. The following headline might have appeared if there were tabloid newspapers in biblical times. You identify the event the headline describes.

MARY'S BROTHER DIES, THEN GETS A RAISE!

_____
_____

Bonus:
In the parable of the beggar and the rich man, who had the same name as Mary's brother?

9. The following sentence contains the hidden name of an Old Testament character. You find the name.

OLD AGE MADE LIL A HAG.

_____
_____

Bonus:
The following sentence contains another hidden name of an Old Testament character. You find the name.

COME TO THE DEMO SESSION.

PLAGUES AND OTHER FUN STUFF

QUIZ #22

10. Rearrange the letters in the word SUNLIT to get what, according to Proverbs, a prudent man ignores.

_____

Bonus:
Rearrange the letters in the word RESIDE to get the word that's missing from this quotation from Job: "Oh, that I might have my request, and that God would grant my _____."

11. John Witherspoon was the only clergyman among the fifty-six men who signed what important American document?

_____

Bonus:
Was John Witherspoon a Presbyterian, Lutheran, or Methodist minister?

12. To whom did Jesus say, "Get thee behind me, Satan"?

_____

Bonus:
To whom did Jesus say, "I am the way and the truth and the life"?

151

Quiz #22: Plagues and Other Fun Stuff

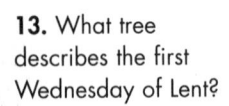

13. What tree describes the first Wednesday of Lent?

14. Which Marx Brother was named for the angelic instrument he played?

15. When Anglicans worship, what is the name of the book they use?

Your Answers:

_____   _____   _____
_____   _____   _____

Bonus: What tree describes a layman in certain Protestant churches who is a spiritual leader and governing officer and sometimes assists the pastor?

Bonus: Early in his career, singer Phil Collins was a member of a rock group named after which book of the Bible?

Bonus: What does a Roman Catholic priest call the book that contains the hymns, prayers, and lessons necessary to enable him to recite the daily "divine office"?

PLAGUES AND OTHER FUN STUFF

INSPIRATION WORD
(9 LETTERS)

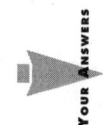

___ ___ ___ ___ ___ ___ ___ ___ ___
 1   2   3   4   5   6   7   8   9

The correct answer to each question begins with one of the letters in the Inspiration Word, and the number in parentheses after the question tells you in which space (above) to insert that letter. Guess each answer and insert its first letter in the proper space. If your answers are right, you'll soon be able to identify the Inspiration Word.

On the *Inspiration, Please!* television show, this Inspiration Word was not guessed until until all nine letters had been revealed.

1. Jacob hid foreign gods and earrings under what kind of tree? (7)
2. According to Greek legend, what king of Thebes unknowingly killed his father and married his mother? (2)
3. The Calvinist doctrine that man's entire nature is corrupt as a result of the fall of Adam and Eve is called what kind of depravity? (5)
4. What Missouri city, called "The Gateway to the West," has the same name as the king who crusaded against the Muslims? (9)
5. The name of the priest who took care of the young Samuel at the Shrine of Shiloh is the same as the first name of a stage and film actor named Wallach. What is the name? (6)
6. It wasn't in Europe, but the six letter word "Europe" contains what ancient two-letter city that was home to Abraham? (3)
7. Name the Hittite who was Bathsheba's first husband. (8)
8. The award-winning song called "Tears in Heaven" was written by what pop singer and composer? (1)
9. The pope's jewelry includes a cross of gold and a fisherman's . . . what? (4)

153

Answers to Quiz #22

Plagues and Other Fun Stuff

1. Gnats, flies, and locusts
2. Adam's apple
3. Ten
4. Golgotha
5. Five
6. Susan B. Anthony (The Susan B. Anthony silver dollar did not find favor with the public.)
7. Laugh
8. Lazarus, the brother of Mary, is raised from the dead by Jesus.
9. Old age maDE LIL A Hag. (Delilah)
10. Insult
11. The Declaration of Independence
12. Peter
13. Ash (Ash Wednesday is the first day of Lent.)
14. Harpo
15. The Book of Common Prayer

Answers to Bonus Questions:

1. Blood
2. The Apple of Discord or The Golden Apple
3. They can have more than one husband.
4. Skull
5. Numbers
6. The other side
7. Sleep
8. The beggar
9. Come to the deMO SESsion. (Moses)
10. Desire
11. Presbyterian
12. Thomas
13. Elder
14. Genesis
15. Breviary

Inspiration Word Answers

1. Oak
2. Oedipus
3. Total
4. St. Louis
5. Eli
6. Ur
7. Uriah
8. (Eric) Clapton
9. Ring

And the Inspiration Word is:

C O U R T E O U S
1 2 3 4 5 6 7 8 9

Quiz #23

HERETIC, THERE A TIC

1. Name the 350-year period of Church-sponsored investigations and trials of heretics that began in Spain in the fifteenth century.

2. Members of the international fraternal organization called the Knights of Columbus are of what religion?

3. "Patriarch of the West" is one of the spiritual titles of whom?

Bonus: Rodrigo Díaz de Vivar, a Spanish hero of the war against the Moors, fought for anyone who hired him, whether Christian or Moor. By what name was he better known?

Bonus: What is the oldest and largest international Jewish service organization?

Bonus: What word describes a man who was an illegitimate claimant to the papal throne?

Quiz #23 — HERETIC, THERE A TIC

4. Spelled one way, it's the last name of a star of silent films. Spelled another way, it's a clergyman attached to a military unit. What is it?

5. What act of servitude did Jesus perform before the Last Supper?

6. What American Virgin Island has the same name as the "doubting" apostle?

Your Answers:

_____

_____

_____

Bonus:
Spelled one way, it's a chicken ready for breading. Spelled another way, it's a Dominican or Franciscan monk. What is it?

Bonus:
Which of Jesus' disciples refused to take part in that act of servitude?

Bonus:
What American Virgin Island has the same name as the apostle credited with writing the Book of Revelation?

156

HERETIC, THERE A TIC

Quiz #23

7. Following are three phrases, including one from the Bible. Each phrase has the same word missing. You fill in the missing word.

____ sale

____ extinguisher

The ____ is not quenched

8. The following headline might have appeared if there were tabloid newspapers in Biblical times. You identify the event the headline describes.

"BARRY" GOES FREE!
P. P. PARDONS CROOK
TO APPEASE ANGRY MOB

9. The following sentence contains the hidden name of one of Jesus' apostles. You find the name.

FOR HOURS I WRITE AND REWRITE.

_____

_____

_____

Bonus:
Following are three more phrases, including one from the Bible, and each with the same word missing. You fill in the missing word.

____ solstice

Like snow in ____

____ of '42

Bonus:
The angry mob in the above headline demanded that "Barry" be freed instead of what man?

Bonus:
The following sentence contains the hidden name of another of Jesus' apostles. You find the name.

DON'T AIM AT THE WINDOW.

Quiz #23: HERETIC, THERE A TIC

10. Rearrange the letters in the word MALES to get an ancient city in Cannan.

11. What one-time prisoner converted to Islam in 1948 and went on to become an outspoken advocate for Black America?

12. Garrison Keillor will tell you that Pastor Ingqvist and Father Emil are ministers in what fictional town?

Bonus: Rearrange the letters in the word SHADE to get a place inhabited by departed souls.

Bonus: After he was sent to jail as a result of the Watergate scandals, who began a Christian ministry for prisoners?

Bonus: In what Broadway musical are all Jews ordered by the tsar to evacuate their homes in the village of Anatevka?

HERETIC, THERE A TIC

Quiz #23

13. What Protestant denomination has its roots in the Scottish branch of the Reformation?

14. When someone talks about the "Bible Belt," is he referring to an item of clothing, a part of the country, or a drink after church?

15. In what way is Pope John Paul II unlike all the other popes since the year 1523?

Bonus:
In the seventh and eighth centuries, the Parsis came to what country to escape persecution?

Bonus:
Salt Lake City, Utah, houses the headquarters of what church founded in the United States by Joseph Smith?

Bonus:
In the 1960s, Pope Paul VI was the first pope in history to travel in what?

QUIZ #23

HERETIC, THERE A TIC

INSPICATION WORD
(8 LETTERS)

YOUR ANSWERS

___ ___ ___ ___ ___ ___ ___ ___
 1   2   3   4   5   6   7   8

The correct answer to each question begins with one of the letters in the Inspiration Word, and the number in parentheses after the question tells you in which space (above) to insert that letter. Guess each answer and insert its first letter in the proper space. If your answers are right, you'll soon be able to identify the Inspiration Word.

On the *Inspiration, Please!* television show, this Inspiration Word was not guessed until all eight letters had been revealed.

1. By what name do Christians refer to the Sunday before Easter? (5)
2. Exodus tells us that an animal shall be stoned when it gores a man or woman to death. What animal? (2)
3. At a traditional Passover meal, a glass of wine is poured and a door left open for what prophet? (7)
4. What apostle gave his name to the city that is the twin of Minneapolis? (4)
5. What relationship was Ruth to Naomi? (8)
6. July 6 is a day of celebration honoring what Tibetan spiritual leader? (3)
7. Fill in the blank in this quote from Matthew: "But I say to you, love your _____, and pray for those who persecute you." (6)
8. Royalties from what Irving Berlin song go to the Boy Scouts of America and Girl Scouts of America? (1)

160

Answers to Quiz #23

Heretic, There a Tic

1. The Spanish Inquisition
2. Roman Catholic
3. The pope
4. (Charles) Chaplin/Chaplain
5. He washed the feet of his disciples.
6. St. Thomas
7. Fire
8. Barabbas, a condemned criminal, is pardoned by Pontius Pilate.
9. For hours I write AND REWrite. (Andrew)
10. Salem
11. Malcolm X
12. Lake Woebegone
13. Presbyterianism
14. A part of the country. (It's the part known for its "Bible-believing" tradition.)
15. He's not Italian. (He's Polish.)

Answers to Bonus Questions:

1. El Cid or The Cid
2. B'nai B'rith
3. Antipope
4. Fryer/friar
5. Peter
6. St. John
7. Summer
8. Jesus
9. Don't aiM AT THE Window. (Matthew)
10. Hades
11. Charles "Chuck" Colson
12. *Fiddler on the Roof*
13. India
14. The Mormon Church or The Church of Jesus Christ of Latter-day Saints
15. An airplane

Inspiration Word Answers

1. Palm Sunday
2. Ox
3. Elijah
4. St. Paul
5. Daughter-in-law
6. Dalai Lama
7. Enemy or enemies
8. "God Bless America"

And the Inspiration Word is:

G O D S P E E D
1 2 3 4 5 6 7 8

QUIZ #24

ANY WAY YOU SLICE IT (OR CUBIT)

1. Noah's ark measured 300 cubits by 50 cubits by 30 cubits. Was a cubit based on the length of a ram's horn, a horse's leg, or a man's forearm?

2. Which of the five books of Moses takes the form of farewell speeches?

3. What word describes the ritual by which devils are expelled?

Bonus:
According to Genesis, Noah built the ark of what kind of wood?

Bonus:
Does that book contain three, twelve, or forty of Moses' farewell speeches?

Bonus:
In Jewish folklore, what word describes a demon—or the soul of a dead person—that enters the body of a living person and controls him?

Any Way You Slice It (or Cubit)

4. On *Saturday Night Live*, Dana Carvey made what female character famous with the catchphrase, "Could it be . . . Satan?"

5. What Christmas carol includes the line, "'Tis the season to be jolly"?

6. The paper on which parts of the Old and New Testaments were written was made from what plant?

Bonus: In the film *True Confessions*, what Oscar-winning actor played a priest?

Bonus: How many times does the word "Christmas" appear in the song "Jingle Bells"?

Bonus: Parts of the Bible also were written on what material made from the skin of sheep and goats?

Quiz #24 — ANY WAY YOU SLICE IT (OR CUBIT)

7. Following are three phrases, including one from the Bible. Each phrase has the same word missing. You fill in the missing word.

Like the ____ of grass

____ child

____ *Drum Song*

8. The following headline might have appeared in a tabloid newspaper in 1208. You identify the event the headline describes.

FRANK'S NEW ORDER
FINDS JOY BELOW
THE POVERTY LEVEL

9. The following sentence contains the hidden name of a biblical character. You find the name.

AT PUBLIC BATHS
HE BALKS.

Bonus:
Following are three phrases, including one from the Bible, and each with the same word missing. You fill in the missing word.

____ gauge shotgun

____ *Angry Men*

At the gates, ____ angels

Bonus:
In his "Canticle of the Sun," the "Frank" in the headline above wrote of the sun and the moon as if they were relatives. What did he call them?

Bonus:
The following sentence contains the hidden name of another biblical character. You find the name.

HE GAVE THE TSAR A
HARD TIME.

164

Any Way You Slice It (or Cubit)

10. Rearrange the letters in the word DOME to get the name of an ancient kingdom that's mentioned in the Bible.

11. On which day of Creation did God create living creatures?

12. During World War II, what teenage Dutch girl wrote a diary while hiding from the Nazis in an attic?

Bonus:
Rearrange the letters in the word DRONE to get the name of the town where King Saul consulted a witch.

Bonus:
God worked on separating the dark from the light on the first day and on what other day?

Bonus:
In what European city will you find that teenage girl's museum?

Quiz #24: Any Way You Slice It (or Cubit)

13. According to mythology, the child of Tethys and Oceanus was what river of the underworld?

14. At the end of the fourth century, Saint Jerome prepared what authorized Latin version of the Bible?

15. What word, used to describe a pastor's congregation, also describes a farmer's herd of sheep?

Bonus: According to the book of Psalms, it was by the waters of what city that "We sat down, yeah, we wept, when we remembered Zion"?

Bonus: The Codex Sinaiticus is a Bible in the British Museum. Why is it noteworthy?

Bonus: Is the part of a church called the "chancel" usually reserved for the choir, the clergy, or the parishioners?

166

ANY WAY YOU SLICE IT (OR CUBIT)

INSPIRATION WORD
(8 LETTERS)

___ ___ ___ ___ ___ ___ ___ ___
 1   2   3   4   5   6   7   8

YOUR ANSWERS

The correct answer to each question begins with one of the letters in the Inspiration Word, and the number in parentheses after the question tells you in which space (above) to insert that letter. Guess each answer and insert its first letter in the proper space. If your answers are right, you'll soon be able to identify the Inspiration Word.

On the *Inspiration, Please!* television show, this Inspiration Word was guessed after six letters.

1. What order of monks was founded at an abbey in France called La Trappe? (7)
2. According to Matthew and Luke, what is known by its fruit? (2)
3. What word, which means "pertaining to the Gospel and its teachings," comes from the Greek word for "good news"? (4)
4. In mythology they include the Oceanids, the Nereids, and the Dryads, and they're differentiated according to the part of nature they personify. What are they called? (5)
5. Aleph, beth, and gimel are the first three letters of what alphabet? (8)
6. In his first inaugural address, what American president said, "We have nothing to fear but fear itself"? (3)
7. According to the King James version of the Bible, Isaiah said, "How beautiful upon the mountain are the feet of those who preach" what kind of tidings? (6)
8. What date in March is St. Patrick's day? (1)

ANSWERS TO QUIZ #24

ANY WAY YOU SLICE IT (OR CUBIT)

1. A man's forearm. A cubit was about 17 to 21 inches long.
2. Deuteronomy
3. Exorcism
4. The Church Lady
5. "Deck the Halls"
6. Papyrus
7. Flower
8. Saint Francis founds the Franciscan Order, a life of joy and poverty.
9. At public BATHS HE BAlks. (Bathsheba)
10. Edom
11. The fifth
12. Anne Frank
13. The Styx
14. Vulgate
15. Flock

ANSWERS TO BONUS QUESTIONS:

1. Gopher wood
2. Three
3. A dybbuk
4. Robert DeNiro
5. None
6. Parchment
7. Twelve
8. Brother Sun and Sister Moon
9. He gave the (T)SAR A Hard time (Sarah)
10. Endor
11. The fourth day
12. Amsterdam
13. Babylon
14. It's the oldest complete Bible in existence.
15. The clergy

INSPIRATION WORD ANSWERS

1. Trappist
2. A tree
3. Evangelical
4. Nymphs
5. Hebrew
6. (Franklin D.) Roosevelt
7. Good tidings
8. Seventeenth

And the Inspiration Word is:

1	2	3	4	5	6	7	8
S	T	R	E	N	G	T	H

QUIZ #25

STATUES WITHOUT LIMITATIONS

1. The inscription on what statue begins with the words "Give me your tired, your poor"?

2. A bronze statue of Helios, the ancient Greek god of the sun, is also one of the Seven Wonders of the World. What is its more familiar name?

3. Name the body of water, between Israel and Jordan, that won't support plant life but will support anybody who floats in it.

Bonus: The entire inscription is called "The New Colossus." Who wrote it?

Bonus: Another of the Seven Wonders of the World is a temple named for an ancient Greek goddess. Name the temple.

Bonus: Name the body of water in which Jesus was baptized.

Quiz #25 — Statues Without Limitations

4. A popular holiday song is called, "O Tannenbaum." What is a "tannenbaum"?

5. In 1961, Pope John Paul XXIII wrote a letter called "Mater et Magistra." What is such a papal letter called?

6. Despite its name, a "divining rod" has no religious use. What is it?

Your Answers

Bonus: According to the Christmas song that begins "Chestnuts roasting on an open fire," who is "nipping at your nose"?

Bonus: Does the pope write such a letter to his Vatican staff, to his oldest cardinal, or to his bishops?

Bonus: Would you be most likely to buy "divinity" at a flower shop, a candy store, or a cosmetics counter?

170

Statues Without Limitations

Quiz #25

7. Following are three phrases, including one from the Bible. Each phrase has the same word missing. You fill in the missing word.

____ warm

Cool Hand ____

____ alone is with me

8. The following headline might have appeared if there were tabloid newspapers in biblical times. You identify the event the headline describes.

WORKERS SAY "NO COMPRENDO" SO HI-RISE PROJECT FAILS!

9. The following sentence contains the hidden name of a place mentioned in the Bible. You find the place.

HE OWNS NINE VEHICLES.

___

Bonus:
Following are three more phrases, including one from the Bible, and each with the same word missing. You fill in the missing word.

____ tide

A ____ upon the world

The Johnstown ____

Bonus:
Whose descendants started building that "hi-rise project"?

Bonus:
The following sentence contains the hidden name of another place mentioned in the Bible. You find the place.

GIVE BETH ANYTHING SHE WANTS.

171

Quiz #25: Statues Without Limitations

10. Rearrange the letters in the word HEART to get something God created on day one.

11. Which of the seven deadly sins is also the name of an animal?

12. The Salvation Army was founded by what former minister?

Bonus: Rearrange the letters in the word THING to get something else God created on day one.

Bonus: Which of the seven deadly sins is also the last name of a country singer?

Bonus: The Salvation Army was founded in 1865 in what country?

Statues Without Limitations

Quiz #25

13. According to mythology, she was the only one of three Gorgons who was mortal, and she had snakes for hair. Who was she?

14. Name the minister who founded the Christian Broadcasting Network and was, for a time, a candidate for president of the United States?

15. Before Delilah shaved Samson's head, how many times had he cut his own hair?

Bonus: That mortal Gorgon and her sisters were so ugly that anyone who looked at them turned to what?

Bonus: Name the minister who was elected mayor of Atlanta and also served in the Carter administration.

Bonus: After Delilah shaved Samson's head, how did he regain his strength?

Quiz #25

STATUES WITHOUT LIMITATIONS

INSPIRATION WORD
(10 LETTERS)

YOUR ANSWERS

___ ___ ___ ___ ___ ___ ___ ___ ___ ___
 1   2   3   4   5   6   7   8   9   10

The correct answer to each question begins with one of the letters in the Inspiration Word, and the number in parentheses after the question tells you in which space (above) to insert that letter. Guess each answer and insert its first letter in the proper space. If your answers are right, you'll soon be able to identify the Inspiration Word.

On the *Inspiration, Please!* television show, this Inspiration Word was guessed after seven letters.

1. Mardi Gras is the day before Lent. "Mardi" means what day of the week? (7)
2. According to Isaiah, "Let us eat and drink" for we will die *when*? (5)
3. England officially became Protestant again during the forty-five-year reign of what daughter of Henry VIII? (2)
4. Isaac named his son Jacob at birth, but God changed Jacob's name to what? (4)
5. "We have grasped the mystery of the atom and rejected the Sermon on the Mount." Those are the words of a World War II general named Bradley. What was his first name? (9)
6. According to the book of Psalms, idols have what, but do not smell? (10)
7. Many famous paintings depict the angel Gabriel revealing to Mary that she has been chosen to be the mother of Jesus. What is the revelation called? (6)
8. Tennessee Williams's play about a defrocked clergyman is called *The Night of the* . . . what? (8)
9. Fill in the blank in the name of this popular Christmas carol: "It Came upon a ____ Clear." (1)
10. Who was made ruler of Babylon after interpreting a dream that had puzzled the king's wise men? (3)

Answers to Quiz #25

Statues Without Limitations

1. The Statue of Liberty
2. The Colossus of Rhodes
3. The Dead Sea
4. A tree (It's a fir tree often used as a Christmas tree.)
5. Encyclical
6. It's a forked stick used to locate underground water and metal deposits.
7. Luke
8. The Tower of Babel can't be built because of the confusion of languages spoken by the builders.
9. He owns NINE VEHicles. (Ninevah)
10. Earth
11. Sloth
12. William Booth
13. Medusa
14. Pat Robertson
15. None. His hair had never been cut.

Answers to Bonus Questions:

1. Emma Lazarus
2. The Temple of Artemis
3. The Jordan River
4. Jack Frost
5. His bishops
6. A candy store. It's a variety of fudge.
7. Flood
8. Noah's
9. Give BETH ANYthing she wants. (Bethany)
10. Night
11. Pride (The country singer is Charley Pride.)
12. England
13. Stone
14. Andrew Young
15. His hair grew back!

Inspiration Word Answers

1. Tuesday
2. Tomorrow
3. Elizabeth I
4. Israel
5. Omar
6. Noses
7. Annunciation
8. Iguana
9. Midnight
10. Daniel

And the Inspiration Word is:

1	2	3	4	5	6	7	8	9	10
M	E	D	I	T	A	T	I	O	N

Quiz #26

By the Numbers

1. How many of the Ten Commandments begin with the words "Thou shalt not" or "You shall not"?

2. In a football game, when a quarterback throws a long, desperation pass that is up for grabs, it's known by what religious name?

3. The 1984 Nobel Peace Prize went to what South African bishop?

Bonus: How many blessings or beatitudes were pronounced by Jesus in the Sermon on the Mount?

Bonus: What bird that is the name of a pro football player in Philadelphia also is the symbol of Saint John the Evangelist?

Bonus: The 1983 Nobel Peace Prize went to what Polish leader?

By the Numbers

Quiz #26

4. The Dead Sea Scrolls contain some books of the Bible. Are they books of the Old Testament or the New Testament?

5. If a Jewish man tells you he's going to "shul," where is he going?

6. What kind of song in praise of God sounds like a masculine pronoun?

Bonus: The Dead Sea Scrolls were written in two languages. Name one of them.

Bonus: If a Jewish man talks about a "mitzvah," is he referring to an item of clothing, an evil spirit, or a good deed?

Bonus: Which song of that type contains the line "Who wert and art and evermore shall be"?

177

Quiz #26 — By the Numbers

7. Following are three phrases, including one from the Bible. Each phrase has the same word missing. You fill in the missing word.

____ Rogers

The ____ of the Lord

The ____ to win

8. The following headline might have appeared if there were tabloid newspapers in the year 1620. You identify the event the headline describes.

BOAT PEOPLE, IN LOVE WITH P.R., SAY, "WE'LL PRAY OUR WAY!"

9. The following sentence contains the hidden name of a book of the Bible. You find the name.

WE WATCHED GENE SISKEL.

Your Answers

Bonus:
Following are three more phrases, including one from the Bible and each with the same word missing. You fill in the missing word.

Bear false ____

____ an accident

Be a ____ for me.

Bonus:
The first agreement for self-government in America was named for a ship. What was it called?

Bonus:
The following sentence contains the hidden name of another book of the Bible. You find the name.

SHE'S ASKING SHAWN TONIGHT.

By the Numbers — Quiz #26

10. Rearrange the letters in the word HEAL to get the name of Jacob's first wife.

11. In the year 1238, the emperor of Constantinople gave the king of France what relic from Jesus' crucifixion?

12. Name the female African-American author of several autobiographical books including *All God's Children Need Traveling Shoes*.

Bonus: Rearrange the letters in the word BALE to get the name of the Bible's first shepherd.

Bonus: According to a legend, what saint identified the true cross by restoring a corpse to life by its touch?

Bonus: That author recited her own inspirational poem at the inauguration of what American president?

Quiz #26 — BY THE NUMBERS

13. The inscription on the Tomb of the Unknowns includes the phrase "Known but to . . ." whom?

14. What is the first musical instrument mentioned in the Bible?

15. Religious scholars like to probe the Bible. What book of the Old Testament rhymes with the word "probe"?

Your Answers

_____   _____   _____
_____   _____   _____

Bonus: America's first Unknown Soldier to be buried in the tomb was a veteran of what war?

Bonus: Who played that instrument to soothe the distracted spirit of King Saul, whom he would succeed?

Bonus: You don't have to be in a special mood to read the Bible. What book of the New Testament rhymes with the word "mood"?

180

BY THE NUMBERS

INSPIRATION WORD
(10 LETTERS)

YOUR ANSWERS

___ ___ ___ ___ ___ ___ ___ ___ ___ ___
 1   2   3   4   5   6   7   8   9   10

The correct answer to each question begins with one of the letters in the Inspiration Word, and the number in parentheses after the question tells you in which space (above) to insert that letter. Guess each answer and insert its first letter in the proper space. If your answers are right, you'll soon be able to identify the Inspiration Word.

On the *Inspiration, Please!* television show, this Inspiration Word was guessed after seven letters.

1. Sinclair Lewis wrote a novel about an unscrupulous evangelist named Gantry. What was Gantry's first name? (5)
2. In the Harrison Ford film *Witness*, a young boy witnesses a murder. To what Christian sect does the boy belong? (9)
3. The disciple who betrayed Jesus with a kiss was Judas . . . who? (7)
4. Seth was a relative of Enoch. What relative? (3)
5. Which book of the Old Testament contains the census of the Israelites after the exodus from Egypt? (6)
6. One of the Beatitudes says, "Blessed are those who mourn, for they will be . . ." what? (2)
7. According to the Gospel of John, John the Baptist referred to Jesus as what animal of God? (10)
8. To Muslims, Mecca is one of the two most sacred cities. What is the other? (4)
9. Sacred Heart University is in the Constitution State. What state is it? (8)
10. Fill in the blank in this Alexander Pope quote: "To _____ is human, to forgive divine." (1)

QUIZ #26

Answers to Quiz #26

By the Numbers

1. Seven
2. A Hail Mary pass
3. Desmond Tutu
4. The Old Testament
5. To a synagogue ("Shul" is the Yiddish word for synagogue.)
6. Hymn/him
7. Will
8. The Pilgrims land at Plymouth Rock (P.R.) in search of religious freedom.
9. We watched GENE SISkel. (Genesis)
10. Leah
11. The crown of thorns
12. Maya Angelou
13. God
14. The harp
15. Job

Answers to Bonus Questions:

1. Eight
2. Eagle
3. Lech Walesa
4. Hebrew and Aramaic
5. A good deed
6. "Holy, Holy, Holy"
7. Witness
8. The Mayflower Compact
9. She's asKING Shawn tonight. (Kings)
10. Abel
11. Saint Helena
12. Bill Clinton
13. World War I
14. David
15. Jude

Inspiration Word Answers

1. Elmer
2. Amish
3. Iscariot
4. Uncle (Enoch was the son of Cain, who was Seth's brother.)
5. Numbers
6. Comforted
7. Lamb
8. Medina
9. Connecticut
10. Err

And the Inspiration Word is:

1	2	3	4	5	6	7	8	9	10
E	C	U	M	E	N	I	C	A	L

Quiz #27

WOMEN, MEN, AND OTHER CHARACTERS

1. How many books of the Old Testament are named for women?

2. What lawyer defended the right of a teacher named Scopes to teach evolution in a Tennessee school?

3. What is the only papal name to appear on the Zodiac?

Bonus: How many books of the New Testament are named for women?

Bonus: Name the religious Fundamentalist and three-time presidential candidate who assisted the *prosecution* in the Scopes trial.

Bonus: What papal name sounds the most devout and reverent?

Quiz #27 — WOMEN, MEN, AND OTHER CHARACTERS

4. On what TV series did Father Mulcahy offer guidance—and comedy—to the troops?

5. It was from the 45th Psalm that Harley Procter, of Procter and Gamble fame, got the name of what soap that is "99 and 44/100 percent pure"?

6. What 1961 Broadway musical that enjoyed a lengthy 1995 revival with Matthew Broderick includes the song "Brotherhood of Man"?

Bonus:
Name the priest, played by Don Novello, who appeared frequently on *Saturday Night Live*.

Bonus:
What household cleanser, available in powdered and liquid form, took its name from a Greek hero of the Trojan War?

Bonus:
What Off-Broadway musical that has been performed all over the world concerns a group of nuns who put on a show to raise money for a funeral?

WOMEN, MEN, AND OTHER CHARACTERS

QUIZ #27

7. Following are three phrases, including one from the Bible. Each phrase has the same word missing. You fill in the missing word.

By ____ or by earth

____ help us

Seventh ____

8. The following headline might have appeared if there were tabloid newspapers in the year 313 A.D. You identify the event the headline describes.

CONNIE SAYS IT'S OK: FAITH IS NOW LEGIT!

9. The following sentence contains the hidden name of a biblical place. You find the place.

ISN'T THAT BABY LONELY?

Bonus:
Following are three more phrases, including one from the Bible, and each with the same word missing. You fill in the missing word.

____ water

____ Grail

____ ground

Bonus:
"Connie" in the above headline ordered the Greek letters "chi" and "rho" to be marked on his soldiers shields. Why those two letters?

Bonus:
The following sentence contains the hidden name of another biblical place. You find the place.

HER HUSBAND IS SO DOMESTIC.

Quiz #27 — WOMEN, MEN, AND OTHER CHARACTERS

10. Rearrange the letters in the word REACTOR to get another word for God.

11. Three of the apostles were with Jesus at the Transfiguration. Name two of them.

12. Spelled with one "T," it's the head of a monastery. Spelled with two "T's," it's the partner of Costello. What is it?

Your Answers:

_____

_____

_____

Bonus:
Rearrange the letters in the word REGAL to get the word that completes this quote from Galatians: "See with what ____ letters I am writing to you."

Bonus:
Who was known as the apostle to the Gentiles?

Bonus:
Spelled with one "L," it's a high-ranking monk. Spelled with two "L's," it looks like a camel without a hump. What is it?

WOMEN, MEN, AND OTHER CHARACTERS

Quiz #27

13. *The House of the Seven Gables* was written by a man named Hawthorne, whose first name is Hebrew for "gift of God." What was his first name?

14. Theodor Herzl founded what worldwide movement for the establishment of a national Jewish homeland in Palestine?

15. What religious leader recorded two best-selling albums in Latin, one spoken and one sung?

_____
_____

_____
_____

_____
_____

Bonus:
The Canterbury Tales was written by a man named Chaucer, whose first name means "divine peace" in Old French. What was his first name?

Bonus:
Herzl's movement takes its name from the hill on which the palace of David stood. In what city was that hill?

Bonus:
That same religious leader wrote a best-selling book called *Crossing the Threshold of* . . . what?

Quiz #27

WOMEN, MEN, AND OTHER CHARACTERS

INSPIRATION WORD
(8 LETTERS)

YOUR ANSWERS

___ ___ ___ ___ ___ ___ ___ ___
 1   2   3   4   5   6   7   8

The correct answer to each question begins with one of the letters in the Inspiration Word, and the number in parentheses after the question tells you in which space (above) to insert that letter. Guess each answer, and insert its first letter in the proper space. If your answers are right, you'll soon be able to identify the Inspiration Word.

On the *Inspiration, Please!* television show, this Inspiration Word was guessed after seven letters.

1. The International Court of Justice, or World Court, is the principal judicial agency of what international organization? (3)
2. The largest animal that lives on land is sacred in Thailand. What animal is it? (7)
3. English clergyman Jonathan Swift wrote a satiric novel about a traveler to the land of the Lilliputians. What was the traveler's name? (4)
4. The jolly priest in *The Adventures of Robin Hood* is named Friar . . . what? (6)
5. The architectural masterpiece called the Pantheon was used as a church for more than twelve hundred years. You'll find what's left of it in what European city? (8)
6. According to Isaiah, the wolf shall dwell with what animal? (1)
7. What is the more common name for an angel's nimbus? (5)
8. After Jesus was crucified, the man who took his body, wrapped it in a linen sheet, and placed it in a tomb was Joseph of . . . what town? (2)

Answers to Quiz #27

Women, Men, and Other Characters

1. Two: Ruth and Esther
2. Clarence Darrow
3. Leo
4. M*A*S*H
5. Ivory (The 45th Psalm mentions ivory palaces.)
6. *How to Succeed in Business Without Really Trying*
7. Heaven
8. Emperor Constantine legalizes Christianity.
9. Isn't that BABY LONely? (Babylon)
10. Creator
11. Peter, James, and John
12. Abbot/Abbott (Bud Abbott was the comedy partner of Lou Costello.)
13. Nathaniel
14. Zionism
15. Pope John Paul II

Answers to Bonus Questions:

1. None
2. William Jennings Bryan
3. Pius, which is pronounced like pious.
4. Father Guido Sarducci
5. Ajax
6. *Nunsense*
7. Holy
8. "Chi" and "rho" are the first two letters in the Greek spelling of Christ.
9. Her husband is SO DOMestic. (Sodom)
10. Large
11. Paul
12. Lama/llama
13. Geoffrey
14. Jerusalem (The hill is called Zion.)
15. Hope

Inspiration Word Answers

1. United Nations
2. Elephant
3. Gulliver
4. Tuck
5. Rome
6. Lamb
7. Halo
8. Arimathea

And the Inspiration Word is:

L A U G H T E R
1 2 3 4 5 6 7 8

Quiz #28

From Saints to Sinners

1. What saint, one of the greatest theologians and philosophers of the Christian church, is known as the "Angelic Doctor"?

2. Which prophet had a vision of a plumb line that measured the nation of Israel?

3. What famous palace and fortress of the Moorish kings was the last stronghold of the Moors against the Christians in Europe?

Bonus: What saint wrote a defense of Christianity and the Catholic Church called *City of God*?

Bonus: What prophet had a vision of dry bones taking on flesh and life?

Bonus: In what European country will you find that fortress?

190

From Saints to Sinners

4. *A Man Called Peter*, a book about a Scottish clergyman who became chaplain of the United States Senate, was written by the clergyman's wife. What is her name?

5. What African word meaning "God" or "demon" describes the religious beliefs, including sorcery and witchcraft, of many people in the West Indies?

6. According to the Roman Catholic Church, a serious, willfully committed transgression against the law of God, which deprives the soul of divine grace, is called what kind of sin?

Bonus: The same author wrote an inspirational book about her mother's experiences as a young teacher in Appalachia, and it became a television series. What was it called?

Bonus: What Portuguese word meaning "charm" or "sorcery" gave us the word that describes an object that is supposed to have magical powers?

Bonus: According to the Roman Catholic Church, is that kind of sin more or less serious than a venal sin?

From Saints to Sinners

Quiz #28

7. Following are three phrases, including one from the Bible. Each phrase has the same word missing. You fill in the missing word.

_____ seas

_____ men of good repute

_____ dwarfs

8. The following headline might have appeared if there were tabloid newspapers in biblical times. You identify the event the headline describes.

STEVE IS STONED AFTER TRIAL AND BECOMES #1 SUFFERER!

9. The following sentence contains the hidden name of a mythological god. You find the name.

THAT'S THE CUP I DROPPED.

Your Answers

Bonus:
Following are three more phrases, including one from the Bible, and each with the same word missing. You fill in the missing word.

_____ shrinker

_____ of the class

A veil on her _____

Bonus:
There is a day named for "Steve." Is it celebrated the day after Lent, the day after Easter, or the day after Christmas?

Bonus:
The following sentence contains the hidden name of another mythological god. You find the name.

I SUPPOSE I DON'T REGRET IT.

192

From Saints to Sinners — Quiz #28

10. Rearrange the letters in the word ODOR to get what, according to Genesis, sin is couching at.

11. What is the popular name for the spinning dancers of one mystical order of the Islam religion?

12. According to the proverb, is the fruit of the righteous a field of lilies, a sheaf of wheat, or a tree of life?

_____   _____   _____

Bonus:
Rearrange the letters in the word SIRE to get what a clergyman frequently asks his congregation to do.

Bonus:
Do those dancers imitate the movements of the trees, the birds, or the planets?

Bonus:
According to the proverb, does hope deferred make the heart beat, make the heart sick, or make the heart stop?

Quiz #28 — From Saints to Sinners

13. Name the body of congregations and offices that assist the pope in the government and administration of the Catholic Church.

14. Sephardic Jews come primarily from two European countries. Spain is one. Name the other.

15. The scriptures tell many stories of people plotting against each other. Who framed Benjamin by having a gold cup planted in his bags?

Bonus: In 1984, the United States established diplomatic relations with the Vatican after an absence of how many years: 17, 77, or 117?

Bonus: The oldest synagogue existing in the United States is the Touro Synagogue in what New England state?

Bonus: The man who framed Benjamin was falsely accused of rape by whose wife?

FROM SAINTS TO SINNERS

INSPIRATION WORD
(10 LETTERS)

YOUR ANSWERS

___ ___ ___ ___ ___ ___ ___ ___ ___ ___
 1   2   3   4   5   6   7   8   9   10

The correct answer to each question begins with one of the letters in the Inspiration Word, and the number in parentheses after the question tells you in which space (above) to insert that letter. Guess each answer and insert its first letter in the proper space. If your answers are right, you'll soon be able to identify the Inspiration Word.

On the *Inspiration, Please!* television show, this Inspiration Word was guessed after six letters.

1. What animal's furry foot is considered a symbol of good luck? (5)
2. What ballet, with music by Tchaikovsky, is a Christmas season classic? (3)
3. The Priest River is in the Gem State, whose capital is Boise. What state is it? (8)
4. A baptism in which the whole body is submerged in water is called what? (6)
5. Fill in the blank in this quote from Matthew's Gospel: "I was ____ and you clothed me." (10)
6. The tendency to evil that is held to be innate in man and transmitted from Adam is called what kind of sin? (9)
7. The *Salome* associated with Rita Hayworth is a movie. The *Salome* associated with Richard Strauss is what? (2)
8. When Judas Maccabee captured Jerusalem from the Syrians, what did he rededicate? (4)
9. As part of the humiliation he suffered, Jesus was given a crown made of what? (7)
10. According to the popular hymn, in order to exchange it someday for a crown, "I will cling to the old rugged . . ." what? (1)

Answers to Quiz #28

From Saints to Sinners

1. Saint Thomas Aquinas
2. Amos
3. The Alhambra
4. Catherine Marshall
5. Voodoo
6. Mortal sin
7. Seven
8. Saint Stephen is stoned to death and becomes the first Christian martyr.
9. That's the CUP I Dropped. (Cupid)
10. Door
11. Whirling Dervishes
12. A tree of life
13. Curia or Roman Curia (or Curia Romana)
14. Portugal
15. Joseph

Answers to Bonus Questions:

1. Saint Augustine
2. Ezekiel
3. Spain (It's in Granada.)
4. *Christy*
5. Fetish
6. More serious
7. Head
8. The day after Christmas
9. I supPOSE I DON't regret it. (Poseidon)
10. Rise
11. Planets (to ask help from good stars and appease evil ones)
12. It maketh the heart sick.
13. 117
14. Rhode Island (It's in Newport.)
15. Potiphar's wife

Inspiration Word Answers

1. Rabbit
2. *(The) Nutcracker*
3. Idaho
4. Immersion
5. Naked
6. Original sin
7. Opera
8. The Temple
9. Thorns
10. Cross

And the Inspiration Word is:

1	2	3	4	5	6	7	8	9	10
C	O	N	T	R	I	T	I	O	N

Quiz #29

Backward and Forward

1. A palindrome is a word, phrase, or sentence that reads the same forward and backward. Who is the first person in the Bible to have a name that is a palindrome?

2. Name the American clergyman who wrote *The Power of Positive Thinking*.

3. *The Aeneid* was written by Virgil to show that Rome was founded, and became great, in accordance with a divine plan. In what language was it written?

Your Answers

Bonus: What well-known three-word palindrome sounds like the first man introducing himself to a woman?

Bonus: What cardinal of the Roman Catholic Church celebrated the marriage and funeral masses of John F. Kennedy?

Bonus: What language, in use since 1200 B.C., is the most important religious and literary language of India?

Quiz #29 — BACKWARD AND FORWARD

4. What word is used to describe food that is allowed to be eaten in accordance with Jewish dietary or ceremonial laws?

5. In the Bible, she's the woman who married the prophet Hosea. On TV in the 1960s, it was the first name of a character played by Jim Nabors. What name is it?

6. The inscription on the Liberty Bell, "Proclaim liberty throughout all the land and unto all the inhabitants thereof," is from which of the first five books of the Old Testament?

Your Answers

Bonus:
In a restaurant that serves that kind of food, dairy products are not served on the same dishes as what?

Bonus:
In the Bible, he's the man required to accept the legal responsibility for Paul's activities. It's also the first name of the actor who plays "George" on *Seinfeld*. What name is it?

Bonus:
The motto "Annuit Coeptis," meaning "God has favored our undertakings," is on every dollar bill. Is it on the side with Washington's picture or the other side?

198

Backward and Forward — Quiz #29

7. Following are three phrases, including one from the Bible. Each phrase has the same word missing. You fill in the missing word.

Our beloved brother _____

_____ Newman

_____ Bunyan

8. The following headline might have appeared if there were tabloid newspapers in 1741. You identify the event the headline describes.

GEORGE'S COMPOSITION IS A RELIGIOUS "MESS"! KIDS IN THE CHORUS SHOUT "HALLELUJAH!"

9. The following sentence contains the hidden name of a biblical place. You find the place.

WHEREVER WE GO SHE NAPS.

Bonus:
Following are three more phrases, including one from the Bible, and each with the same word missing. You fill in the missing word.

_____ ride

_____ to the world

My _____ fulfilled

Bonus:
Another of "George's" compositions was named for which biblical character: Esther, Jezebel, or Ruth?

Bonus:
The following sentence contains the hidden name of another biblical place. You find the place.

SOME FILM STARS USE NO MAKEUP.

Quiz #29: Backward and Forward

10. Rearrange the letters in the word LAMPS to get a sacred song.

11. According to the proverb, shall a woman who feareth the Lord be humbled, praised, or rewarded?

12. The first name of Miss Hamill, the ice skating star, means "gift of God" in Greek. What is her first name?

Bonus: Rearrange the letters in the word GLEAN to get one of the God's celestial attendants.

Bonus: According to the proverb, is the fear of the Lord the beginning of salvation, peace, or knowledge?

Bonus: The first name of Miss Korbut, the Russian gymnastics star, is Russian for "holy." What is her first name?

Backward and Forward

13. A spiritual leader of Islam called a caliph claims succession from whom?

14. "O that you would kiss me with the kisses of your mouth." Those words are not from a romance novel, but from a book of the Old Testament. What book?

15. What is the name of fourteen popes *and* the first name of Mr. Arnold, the traitor?

Bonus:
In the Shiite religious hierarchy, what title is given to a scholar who demonstrates highly advanced knowledge of Islamic law?

Bonus:
In that Old Testament book, a bride begs the daughters of what biblical city not to stir up or awaken her love?

Bonus:
What is the title of a prelate who oversees local churches or a diocese *and* the last name of Joey, the comedian?

QUIZ #29: BACKWARD AND FORWARD

INSPIRATION WORD
(8 LETTERS)

___ ___ ___ ___ ___ ___ ___ ___
1   2   3   4   5   6   7   8

The correct answer to each question begins with one of the letters in the Inspiration Word, and the number in parentheses after the question tells you in which space (above) to insert that letter. Guess each answer, and insert its first letter in the proper space. If your answers are right, you'll soon be able to identify the Inspiration Word.

On the *Inspiration, Please!* television show, this Inspiration Word was guessed after seven letters.

1. What King of Babylonia dreamed of a huge tree reaching up to the heavens? (5)
2. Luke says to love your enemies, do good and lend, and expect what in return? (3)
3. Baboons, bulls, cats, and crocodiles were all sacred animals in what ancient nation of temples and tombs? (6)
4. What country has the world's largest Hindu population? (2)
5. The name of the capital of New Mexico means "holy faith." Name the capital. (8)
6. Rachel is the first woman in the Bible of her occupation. What occupation was it? (7)
7. He directed many biblical Hollywood epics, including *The Ten Commandments*. What was his name? (4)
8. In some European countries, Santa Claus is called Kris . . . who? (1)

Answers to Quiz #29

Backward and Forward

1. Eve
2. Norman Vincent Peale
3. Latin
4. Kosher
5. Gomer (The Jim Nabors character was "Gomer Pyle.")
6. Leviticus
7. Paul
8. George Handel writes *Messiah*, which includes the "Hallelujah" chorus.
9. Wherever we GO SHE Naps. (Goshen)
10. Psalm
11. Praised
12. Dorothy
13. Muhammad
14. Song of Solomon or Songs of Songs or Canticle of Canticles
15. Benedict

Answers to Bonus Questions:

1. Madam I'm Adam.
2. Richard Cardinal Cushing
3. Sanskrit
4. Meat products
5. Jason
6. The other side (It's part of the Great Seal of the United States.)
7. Joy
8. Esther (Handel's first successful oratorio was named for Esther.)
9. Some film sTARS USe no makeup. (Tarsus)
10. Angel
11. Knowledge
12. Olga
13. Ayatollah
14. Jerusalem
15. Bishop

Inspiration Word Answers

1. Nebuchadnezzar
2. Nothing
3. Egypt
4. India
5. Santa Fe
6. Shepherdess
7. (Cecil B.) DeMille
8. Kringle

And the Inspiration Word is:

K	I	N	D	N	E	S	S
1	2	3	4	5	6	7	8

Quiz #30

For Better or Verse

1. The shortest verse in the Bible contains only two words. The first word is "Jesus." What is the second word?

2. In William Golding's novel, the title character is the Lord of the . . . what?

3. What ancient Chinese philosopher taught a system of ethics and education stressing love for humanity, ancestor worship, reverence for parents, and harmony in thought and conduct?

Your Answers

_____

_____

Bonus: Will you find that verse in the Gospel of Matthew, Mark, Luke, or John?

Bonus: In J.R.R. Tolkien's novel, the title character is the Lord of the . . . what?

Bonus: Zoroastrianism, founded by the ancient religious teacher named Zoroaster, is a religion in what middle-eastern country?

204

For Better or Verse — Quiz #30

4. William Miller predicted that Christ would return on October 22, 1844. What Protestant sect grew from Miller's teachings?

5. What is the more common name of the biblical force of nature that is sometimes called "the deluge"?

6. What takes place at a Jewish ceremony called a "bris"?

Bonus: William Miller based his prediction of Christ's return on his reading of which of these three adjacent books of the Old Testament: Daniel, Hosea, or Joel?

Bonus: What sign of nature did God set in the clouds to indicate that he would never again cause a "deluge"?

Bonus: At a bris, it's an honor to be the "sandek." What does the "sandek" hold?

QUIZ #30 — FOR BETTER OR VERSE

7. Following are three phrases, including one from the Bible. Each phrase has the same word missing. You fill in the missing word.

Pin _____

_____ order

_____ for the tax

8. The following headline might have appeared if there were tabloid newspapers in biblical times. You identify the event the headline describes.

SHRUB BURNS AND TALKS: TELLS MO WHERE TO GO!

9. The following sentence contains the hidden name of a book of the Old Testament. You find the name.

THOSE ARE MY FAVORITE SHOES.

Bonus:
Following are three more phrases, including one from the Bible, and each with the same word missing. You fill in the missing word.

_____ iron

He _____ out demons

_____ of characters

Bonus:
Who said to "Mo," "I am that I am"?

Bonus:
The following sentence contains the hidden name of another Old Testament book. You find the name.

WAS P. T. BARNUM BERSERK?

For Better or Verse — Quiz #30

10. Rearrange the letters in the word WARDEN to get the name of one of the twelve apostles.

11. "We should live our lives as though Christ were coming this afternoon." Those words were spoken in March 1976 by what man who was elected president eight months later?

12. Name the Inquisitor General appointed by King Ferdinand and Queen Isabella, under whose direction 2,000 heretics were burned and more than 20,000 Jews were expelled from Spain.

Bonus: Rearrange the letters in the word LEAF to get the tiny animal that David compared himself to when Saul pursued him.

Bonus: "I believe that truth is the glue that holds government together." Those are the words of what man who *lost* the 1976 presidential election?

Bonus: What word, first used in Venice in the sixteenth century, described a part of the city where Jews were sequestered?

207

Quiz #30 — For Better or Verse

13. In the Bible, there are several references to a "denarius." What was a "denarius"?

14. Members of what religion would be most likely to worship the deity called "Vishnu"?

15. The name of what biblical country is Greek for "between the rivers"?

Your Answers

_____   _____   _____

_____   _____   _____

Bonus: In Revelation a denarius is equated to a quart of wheat or three quarts of what?

Bonus: Is Vishnu's wife, the Goddess of Fortune, usually pictured holding a dove, an apple, or a lotus?

Bonus: Name the two rivers between which that biblical country was located.

FOR BETTER OR VERSE

QUIZ #30

INSPIRATION WORD
(10 LETTERS)

YOUR ANSWERS

__ __ __ __ __ __ __ __ __ __
1 2 3 4 5 6 7 8 9 10

The correct answer to each question begins with one of the letters in the Inspiration Word, and the number in parentheses after the question tells you in which space (above) to insert that letter. Guess each answer and insert its first letter in the proper space. If your answers are right, you'll soon be able to identify the Inspiration Word.

On the *Inspiration, Please!* television show, this Inspiration Word was guessed after seven letters.

1. What famous antislavery novel was written by Harriet Beecher Stowe? (7)
2. In the Pledge of Allegiance, what word follows "one nation, under God"? (4)
3. Moses commanded the waters of what sea to part? (3)
4. Emperor Constantine established the time in spring for observing what Christian holiday? (9)
5. It is observed as a day of rest and religious observation by most Christians on Sunday and by most Jews on Saturday. What is it called? (10)
6. Fill in the blank in the title of Martin Scorcese's controversial film about Jesus: *The Last _____ of Christ.* (6)
7. On what mount did Elijah confront and destroy the 450 prophets of Baal? (2)
8. A special evangelical service devoted to a religious awakening, and characterized by the intense worship of the participants, is called what kind of meeting? (8)
9. In Revelation, it's one of the "seven churches of Asia." Today it's what city in Pennsylvania? (5)
10. Zacchaeus managed to get a good look at Jesus by running ahead and climbing up into what kind of tree? (1)

209

Answers to Quiz #30

For Better or Verse

1. Wept
2. Flies
3. Confucius
4. Seventh-day Adventists
5. The flood
6. An infant boy is circumcised.
7. Money
8. Through a burning bush, God tells Moses to go to Egypt and tell Pharaoh to "let my people go."
9. (T)HOSE Are my favorite shoes. (Hosea)
10. Andrew
11. Jimmy Carter
12. Torquemada
13. A coin or monetary unit
14. Hinduism
15. Mesopotamia

Answers to Bonus Questions:

1. John
2. Rings
3. Iran
4. Daniel
5. A rainbow
6. The baby being circumcised
7. Cast
8. God
9. Was P. T. BarNUM BERSerk? (Numbers)
10. Flea
11. Gerald Ford
12. Ghetto
13. Barley
14. A lotus
15. The Tigris and the Euphrates

Inspiration Word Answers

1. *Uncle Tom's Cabin*
2. Indivisible
3. The Red Sea
4. Easter
5. Sabbath
6. Temptation
7. Carmel
8. Revival
9. Philadelphia
10. Sycamore

And the Inspiration Word is:

1	2	3	4	5	6	7	8	9	10
S	C	R	I	P	T	U	R	E	S

About the Editors

Donald K. Epstein, the creator and producer of *Inspiration, Please!* on the Odyssey Channel, is a veteran television producer and writer who specializes in game shows and "event" entertainment specials. Since the early 1970s, he has produced dozens of TV game shows—from *Three on a Match,* a true-or-false quiz hosted by Bill Cullen, to *Jackpot,* a riddle game played by fifteen contestants at once—and written more than 50,000 game-show questions. He also has provided the scripts for scores of awards shows, beauty pageants, and musical specials. The *Country Music Awards* on CBS, which he's scripted for more than twenty years, was called by *TV Guide* "the model to which every televised awards show should aspire." His recent credits include a two-hour musical tribute to comedienne Minnie Pearl and *Hats Off to America,* a holiday special hosted by Larry Hagman. In addition to his television work, Don has produced and written the books and lyrics for more than a score of musical industrial shows for Pepsico, Minolta, Eastman Chemical, and many other major corporations.

Linda Hanick, executive producer of *Inspiration, Please!,* is the director of television production for the Parish of Trinity Church in New York City, where she is responsible for the development and production of a wide variety of programs, as well as the management of Trinity's television facility. The many programs she has produced include the dramatic series *Trinity*

About the Editors

Playhouse, Discovering Everyday Spirituality with Thomas Moore, Wrestling with Angels, Heroes of Conscience, hosted by Bill Moyers, and *Celebrating the Spirit with Garrison Keillor.* She is currently overseeing the production of *Pioneers of the Spirit,* a biography series on the lives of the mystics, and *The Spirituality of Children,* a two-hour special featuring traditional, ordinary, and extraordinary ways in which one can nurture the spiritual life of youngsters. Linda has received many awards for her work, including four New York Emmy Awards, the American Film Festival's Blue Ribbon, the CINE Gold Eagle, and a Cable Ace nomination. She lives in Brooklyn Heights, New York.

If You'd Like to Be A Contestant

Auditions for contestants for the *Inspiration, Please!* television program are held several times a year in New York City, where the show is taped. Auditions are informal and fun.

If you live in the greater metropolitan New York area, and would like to audition, please send a postcard with your name, address, *and* daytime *and* nighttime telephone numbers to:

Inspiration, Please!
Trinity Productions
74 Trinity Place—4th Floor
New York, N.Y. 10006

Our contestant coordinators will call you as soon as our next auditions are scheduled.

About Trinity Church

Inspiration, Please! is produced by the Parish of Trinity Church in New York City. Situated in the heart of the financial district at the intersection of Wall Street and Broadway, Trinity's television department also produces documentaries, dramas, and talk shows. Broadcast on Odyssey and PBS, Trinity productions have been honored with numerous awards including five local New York Emmys, the Red and Blue Ribbons of the American Film Festival, and a Cable Ace nomination.

Trinity Church was founded in 1697 and was granted a large portion of land in lower Manhattan by Queen Anne of England. Over the past three hundred years, through its Grants Program and other activities, Trinity has provided the land or funding for more than seventeen hundred institutions in the United States, including Columbia University, and was instrumental in the support of the work of Desmond Tutu in South Africa. Memorable personalities involved from Trinity's past include George Washington, a member of the congregation, Alexander Hamilton and Robert Fulton, who are buried in the churchyard, and Clement Clark Moore, the son of the sixth Rector of Trinity Church and author of "A Visit from St. Nicholas."

About Odyssey

Odyssey is a broad-based interfaith cable television channel that presents religious, faith, and values programming. Odyssey's programming includes worship, family entertainment, documentaries, music, debate, health and lifestyles, spirituality, relationships, and children's programming. *Inspiration, Please!*, which airs daily on Odyssey, is television's first religious game show.

Odyssey is jointly owned by VISN Management Corp., a subsidiary of the National Interfaith Cable Coalition, Inc. (NICC) and Liberty Media Corp., a subsidiary of Tele-Communications Inc. (TCI). The NICC membership is comprised of representatives of over sixty-four faith groups in the United States from the Protestant, Jewish, Roman Catholic, and Eastern Orthodox traditions.

Odyssey is currently available on more than sixteen hundred cable systems nationwide reaching nearly 30 million homes. If your community does not already have Odyssey on its cable system, call the system and request it be added. If you would like more information on the channel call 888-390-7474 or log on to the channel's web site at www.odysseychannel.com.